Coloring Book for Adults
Relaxation & Stress Relieving Patterns

Vol. 18

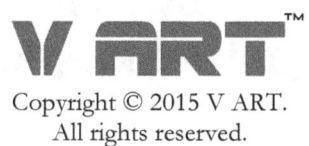

Enjoy All the Benefits of Coloring...

Although coloring books are extremely popular among children, adults all over the world are rediscovering the therapeutic fun of coloring. Here are some of the benefits of this great recreational hobby:

It's a great creative outlet. In everyday life, we're taught to think inside the box. With coloring, we are encouraged to use those creative impulses as we like. The limits are endless!

It reduces stress. If your life is hectic and frantic, coloring is a fabulous method to de-stress and to enhance your relaxation -- all with the simple stroke of a crayon!

It brings people together. Are you stumped for a fun family activity that's appropriate and enjoyable for all ages? Try coloring! It's a great way to bond with the kids in your life.

It enhances mental prowess. Our brains are always growing and evolving throughout our lives. By using your imagination, even for the simple act of coloring, you are keeping your mental skills sharp.

Coloring encourages you to make something beautiful! You pick the colors, you pick the way they are arranged. The finished product can even be proudly displayed in your home or office as a fascinating conversation piece.

Best of all -- it's just plain fun for everyone!

5 Great Ways to Use This Awesome Book

This book is great for fun, meditation, and also for color therapy.

1. You can't do it wrong- You can only do it right!

That is great, isn't it? The designs you will find in this book are made so that you can color them, you can go about this however you like it, you can color inside the lines, or outside the lines, you can also do both, whatever gives you pleasure. You have the choice of choosing whichever pattern or color that you like.

I will also like to inform you that you can use this book for meditation. Here's how:

a. you can select any mandala that calls or attracts you.

b. make your choice of colors, those colors should be those that resonates well with the pattern you have chosen.

c. with joy, begin to color the paper, just flow with it and fill the spaces on each page with color, lines, dots and shapes. You can even use words!

d. Flow with the process! Don't get disconnected.

2. Masculine style mandala coloring

This is an active search for the point of wholeness, of nothingness. Immerse yourself into those patterns, let the noise that's all around you and creating that turmoil fade away, focus on each of the stroke you are making, you will be released as soon as you complete coloring and you will feel refreshed, I guarantee you that.

3. Feminine style mandala coloring

There is an abundance of joy in the world, you've got to find it. This style is a celebration of the abundance of joy. Fill your vision with color. Take pleasure in the caress of your pen. Your fulfillment will be in the process.

4. Make it about someone else

This is very interesting, remember that life is not all about yourself. you can also make this journey about someone else, it will benefit you a great deal. For example: you can choose an important figure to you- like your mother, or father.
Go about coloring it mindfully, as you reflect on every characteristic of such relationship. You will find forgiveness, compassion and understanding. You may even discover a way to celebrate such important relationship. Now, can you just imagine what a blessing that would be? It would be just great.

5. Color therapy

This is also of great advantage for those who need 'color therapy' this book is a very useful tool for color therapy. If a specific chakra requires energy, you have the liberty to select its' color and fill the entire mandala with shades and values of that color.
Now, remember to keep the mandala at a place where it would be very much visible to you, this will help you to focus more on the energies you want to nurture.
Most importantly, mandalas are a wonderful way to enjoy color and quiet doodling for pleasure.
Here is a warning for you: Beware, they are addictive

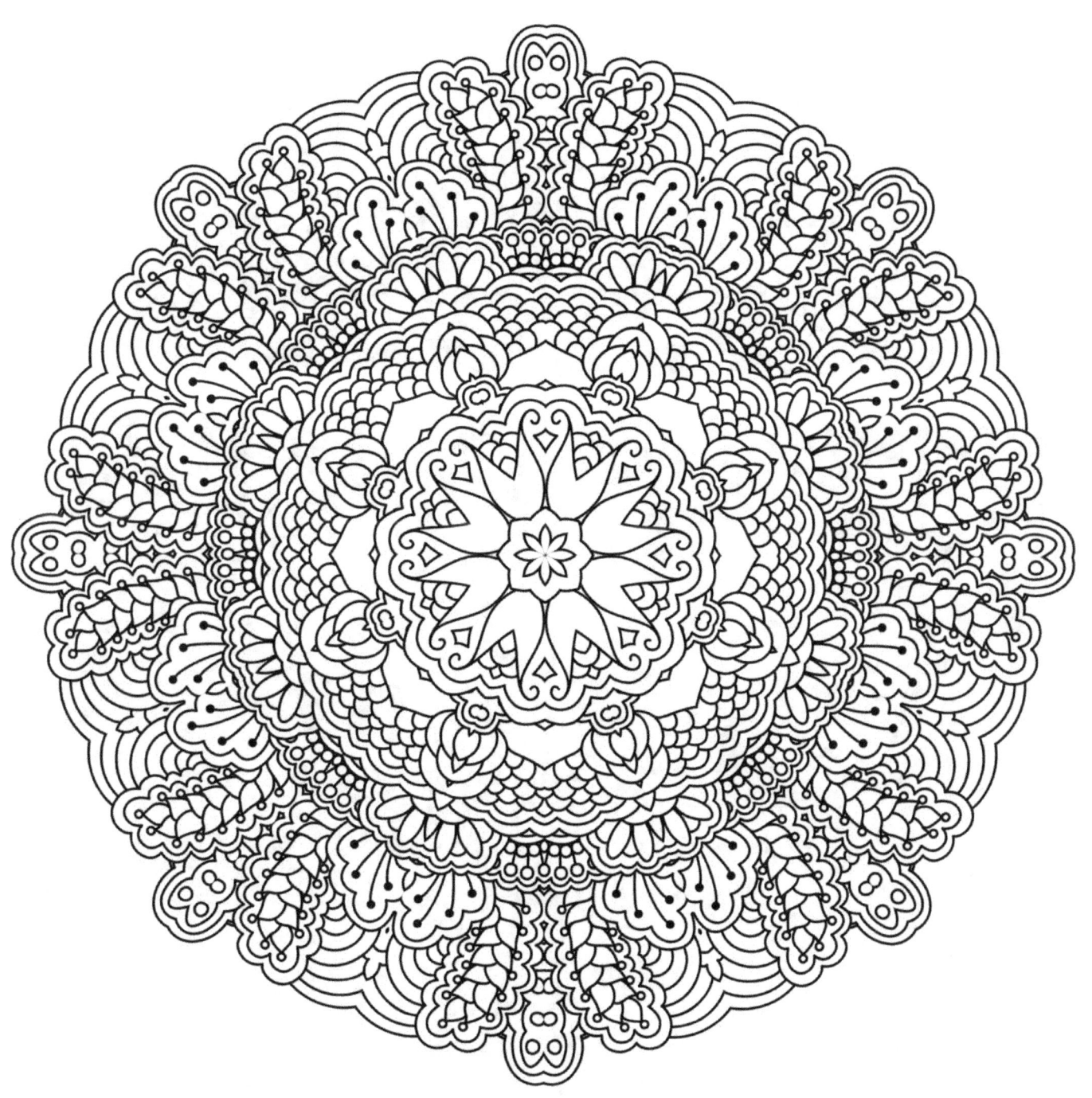

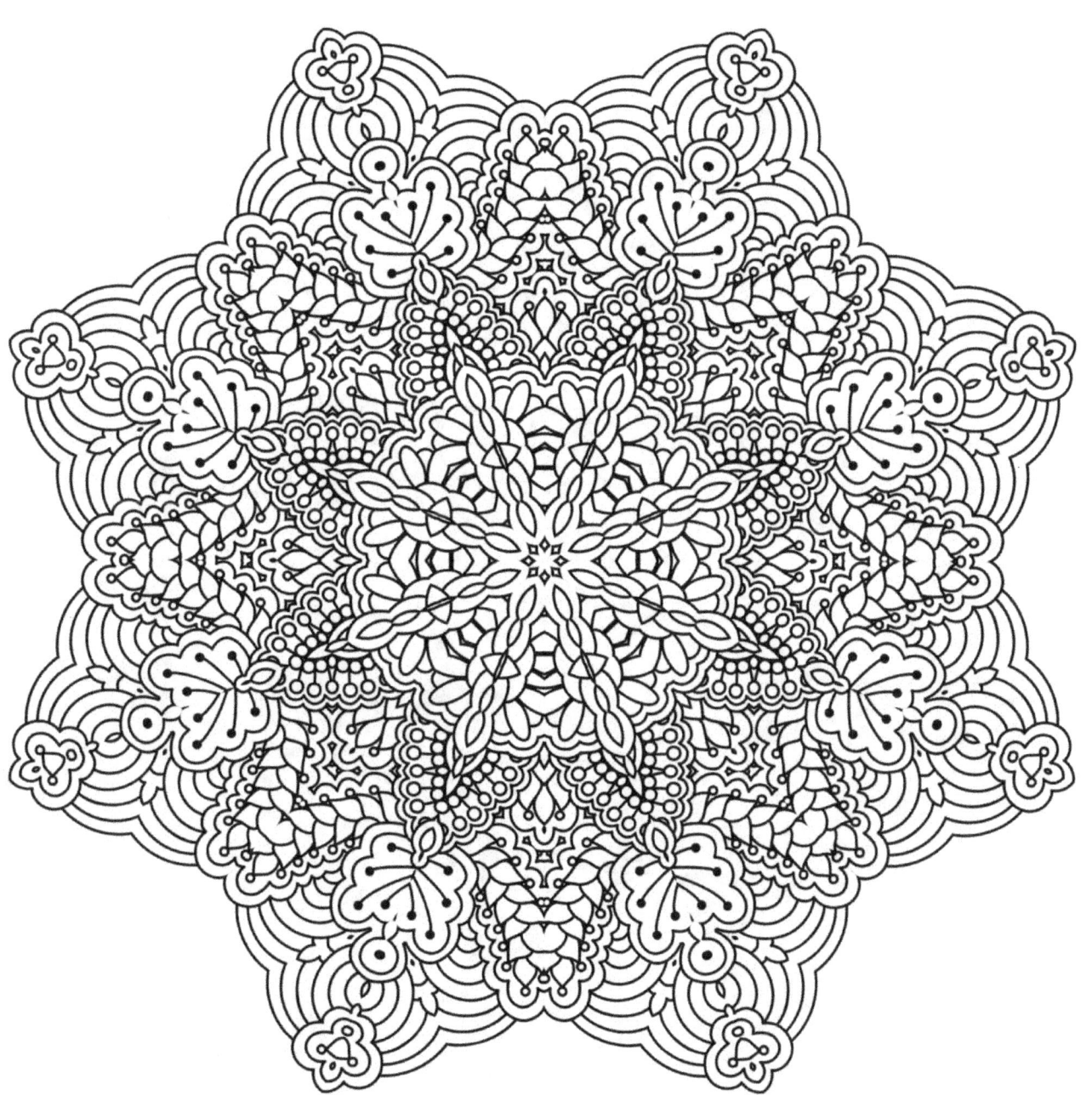

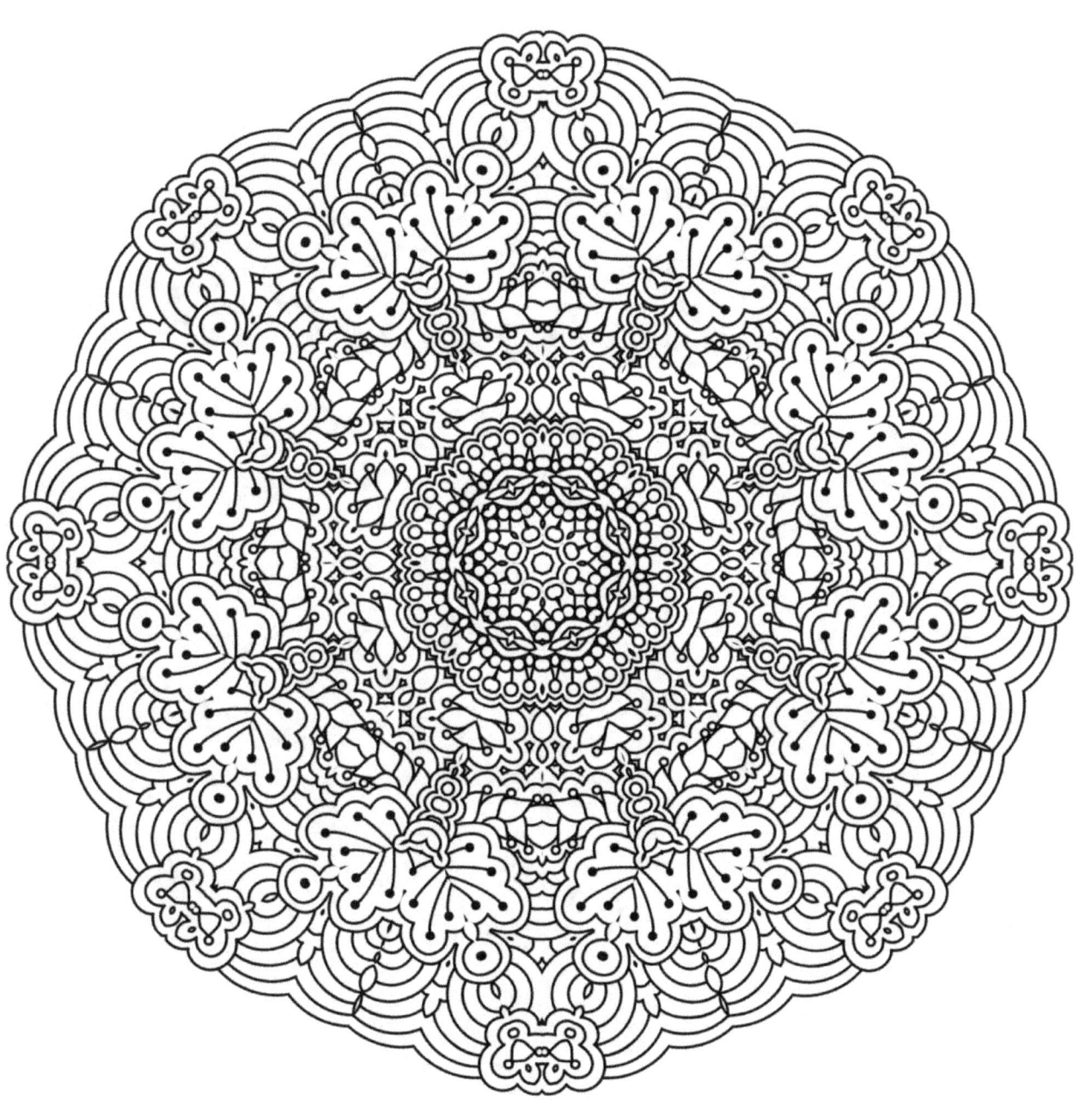

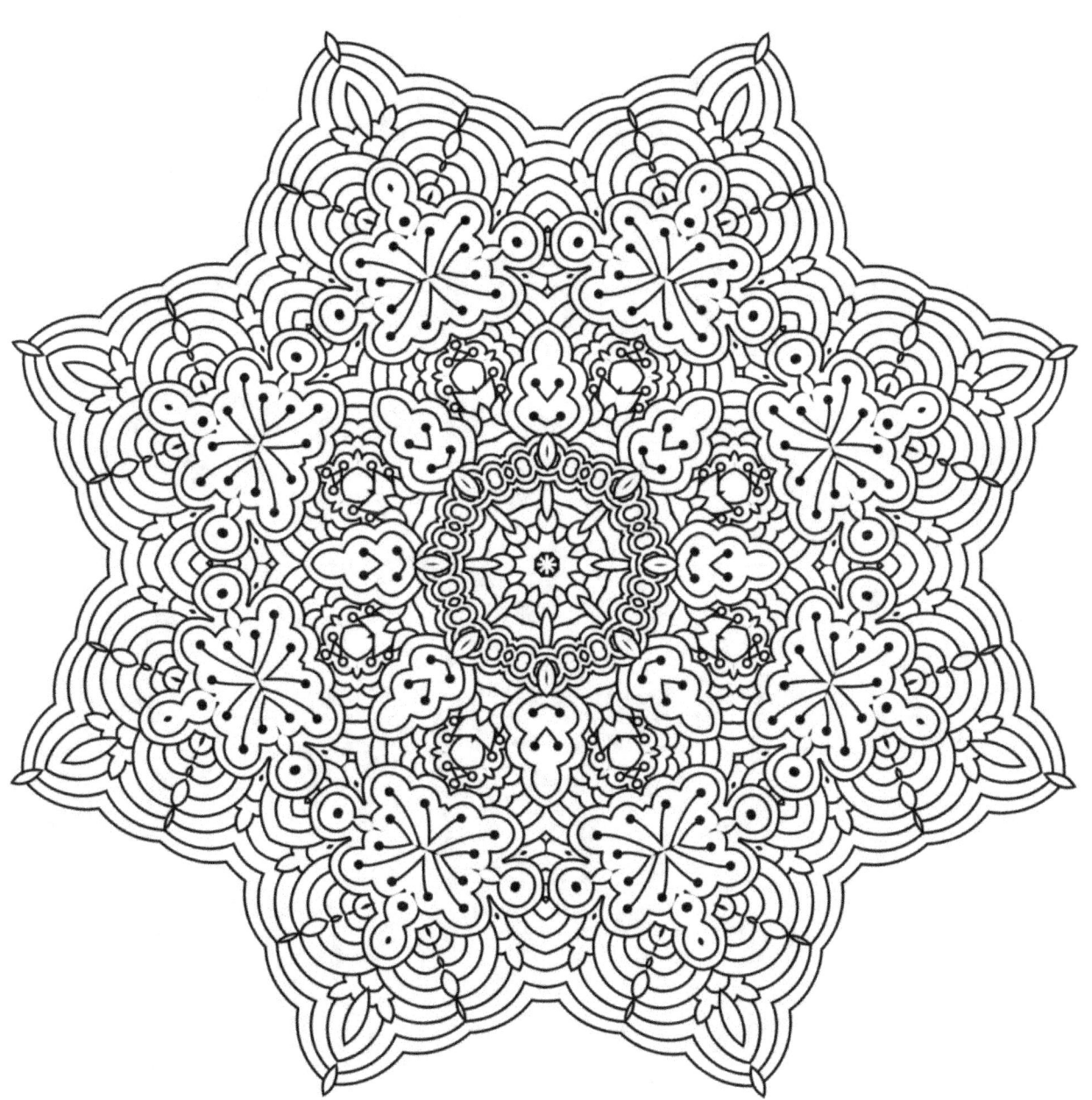

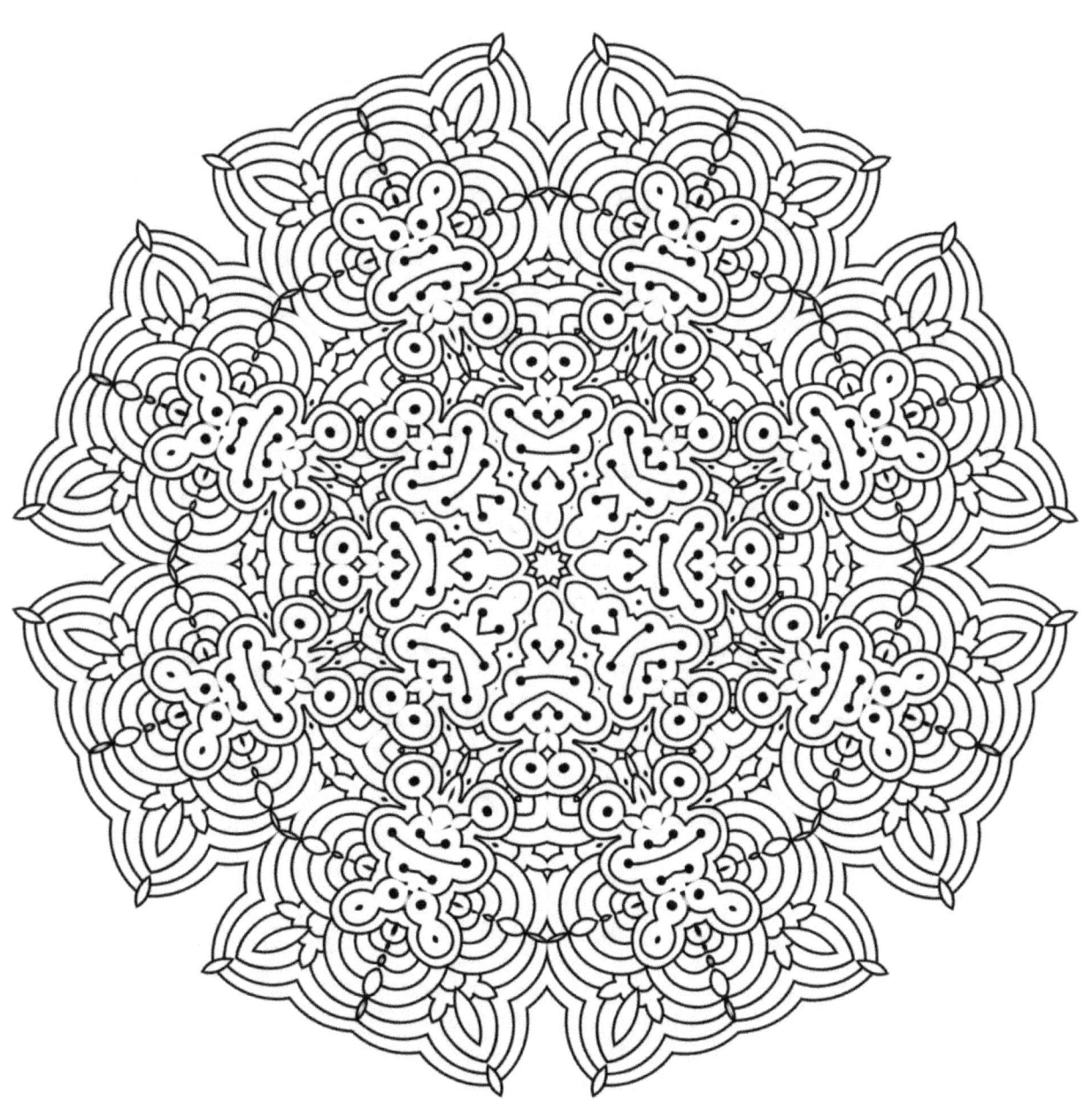

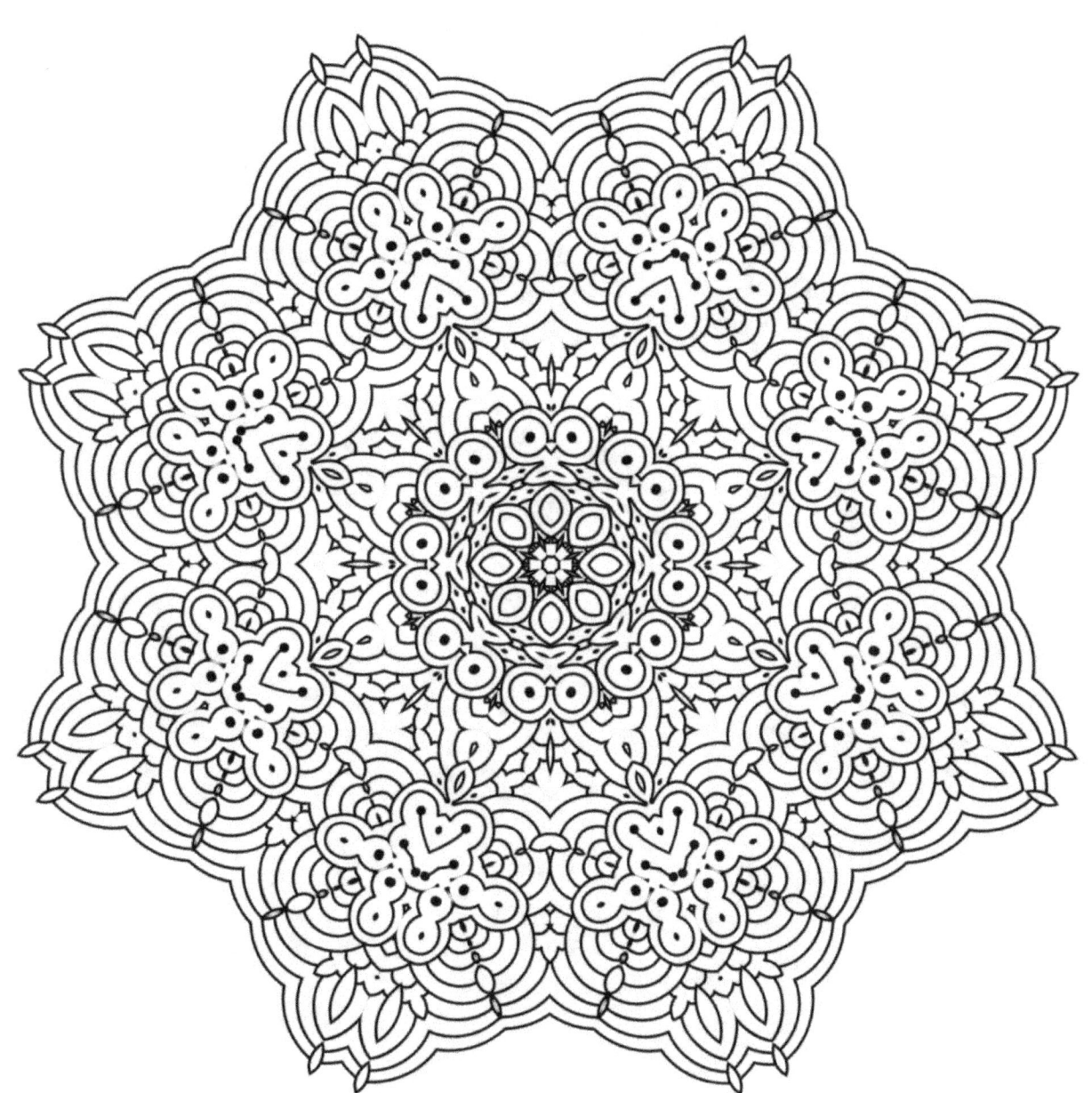

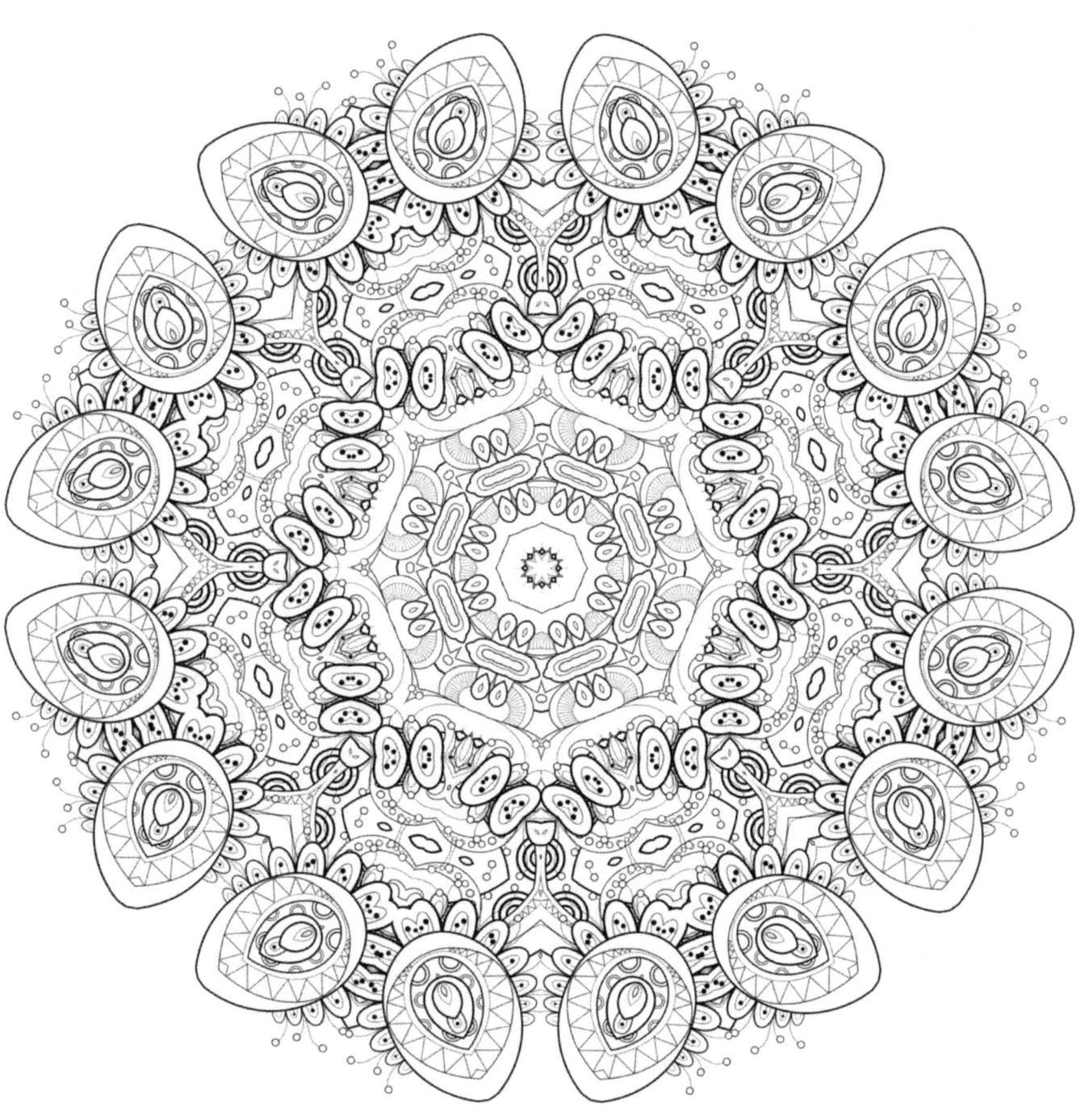

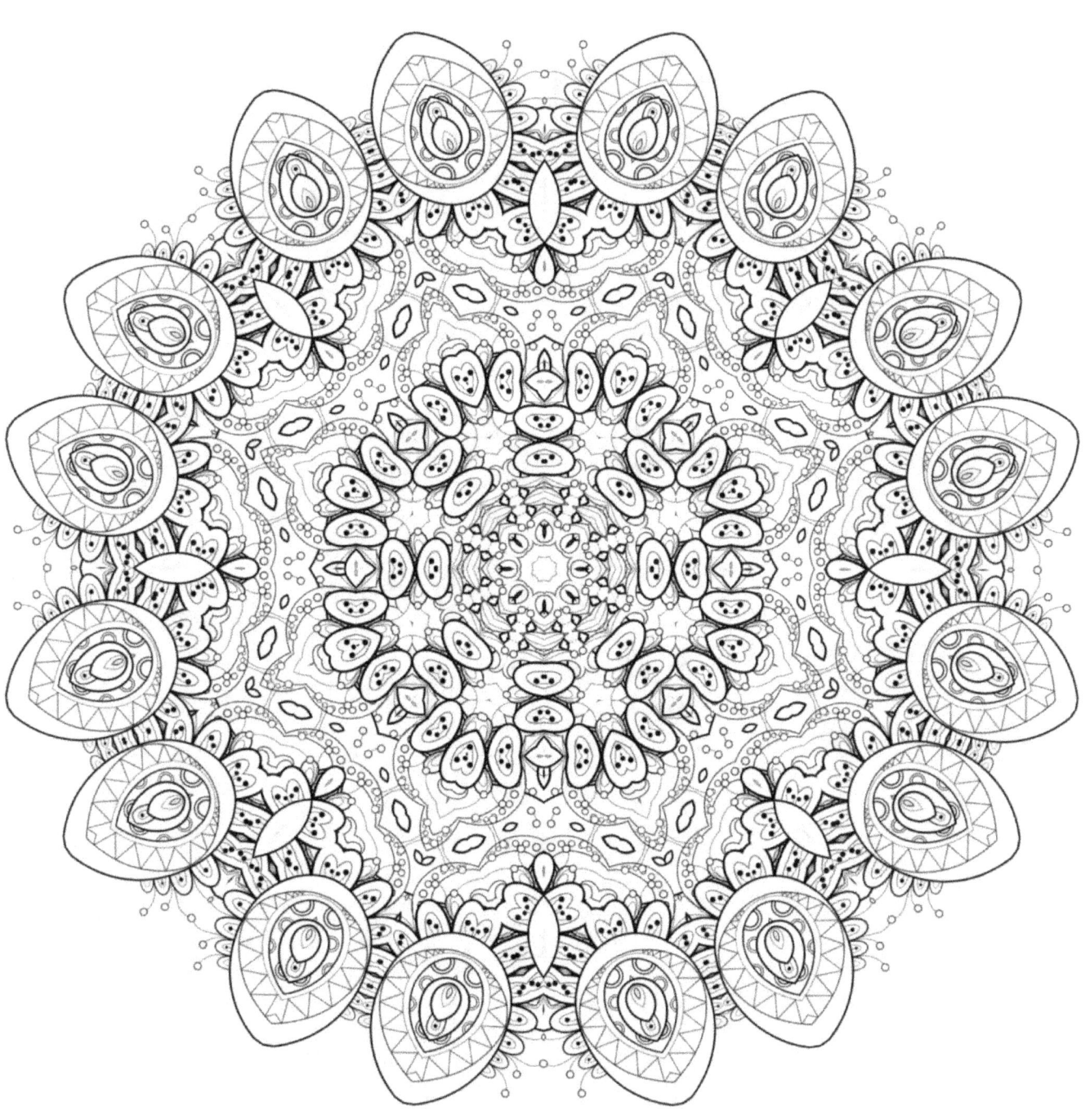

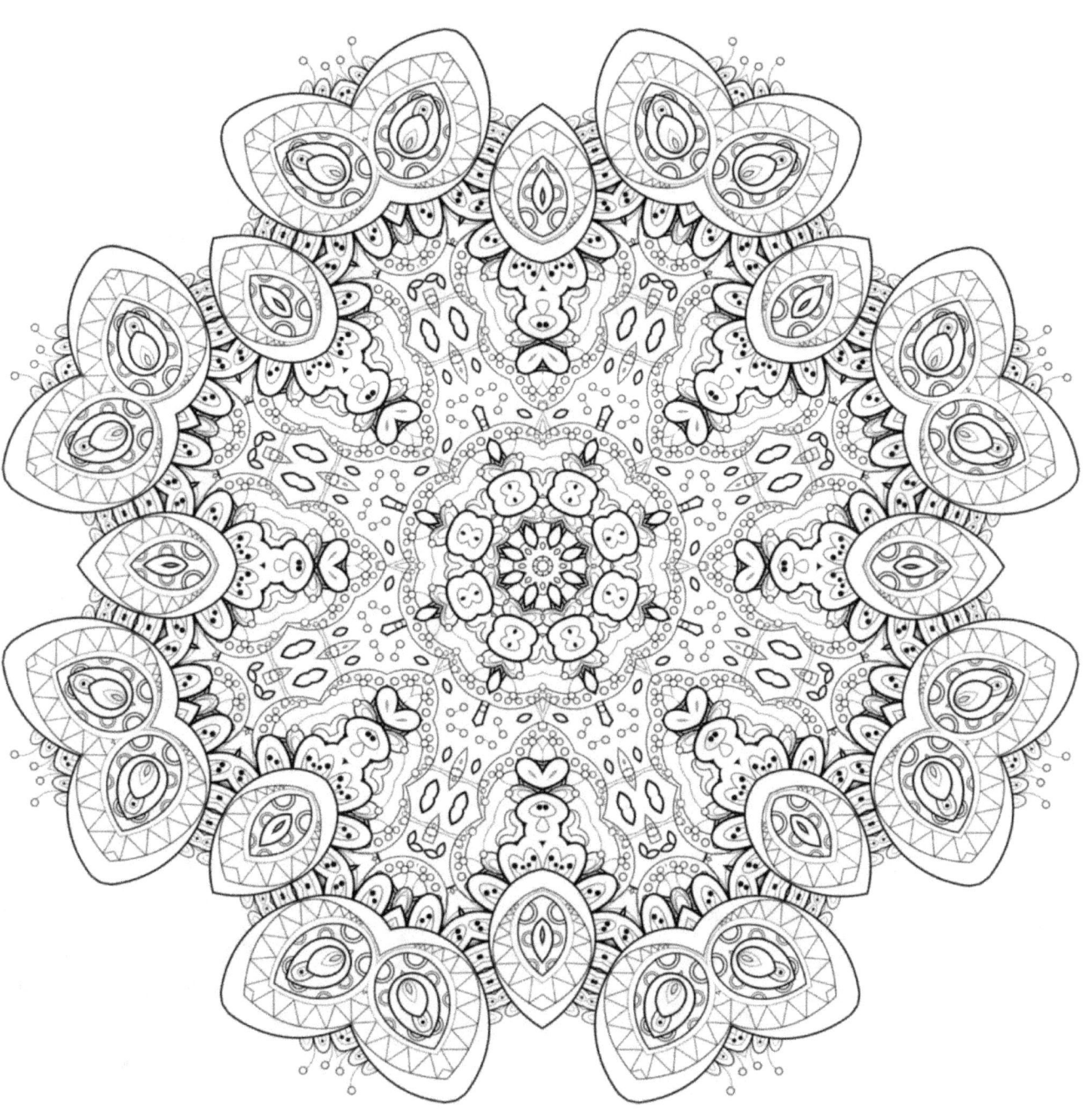

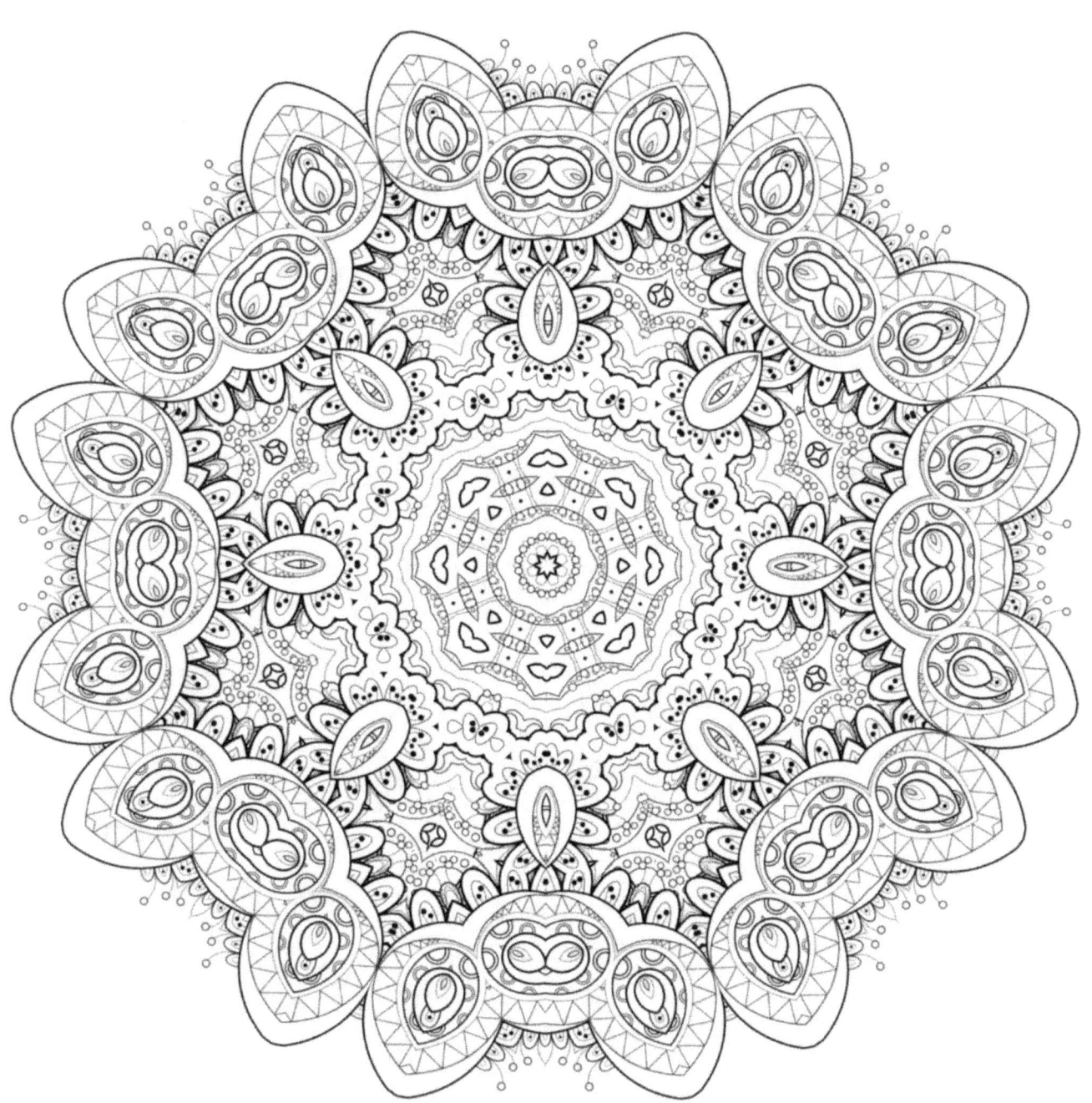

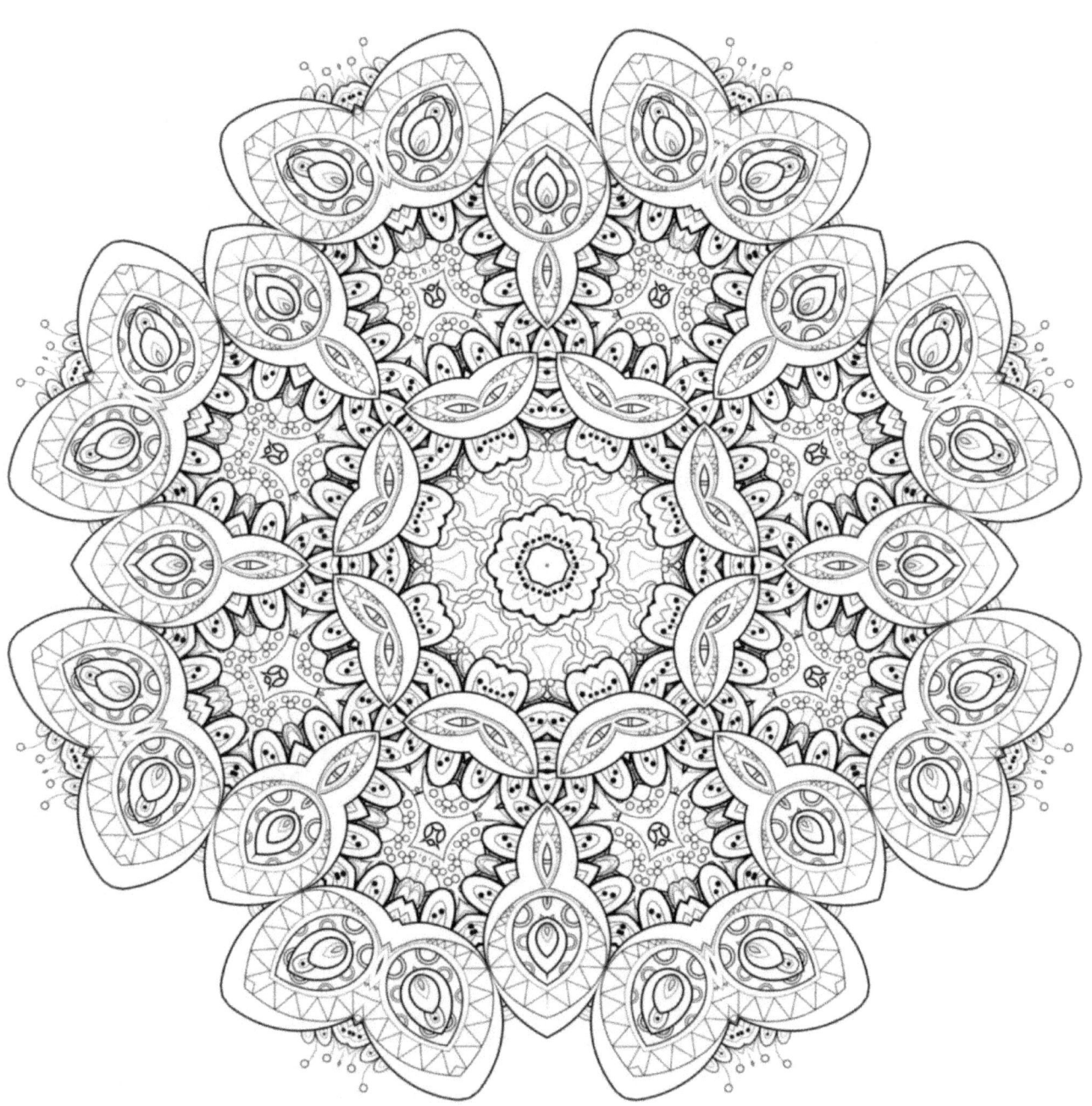

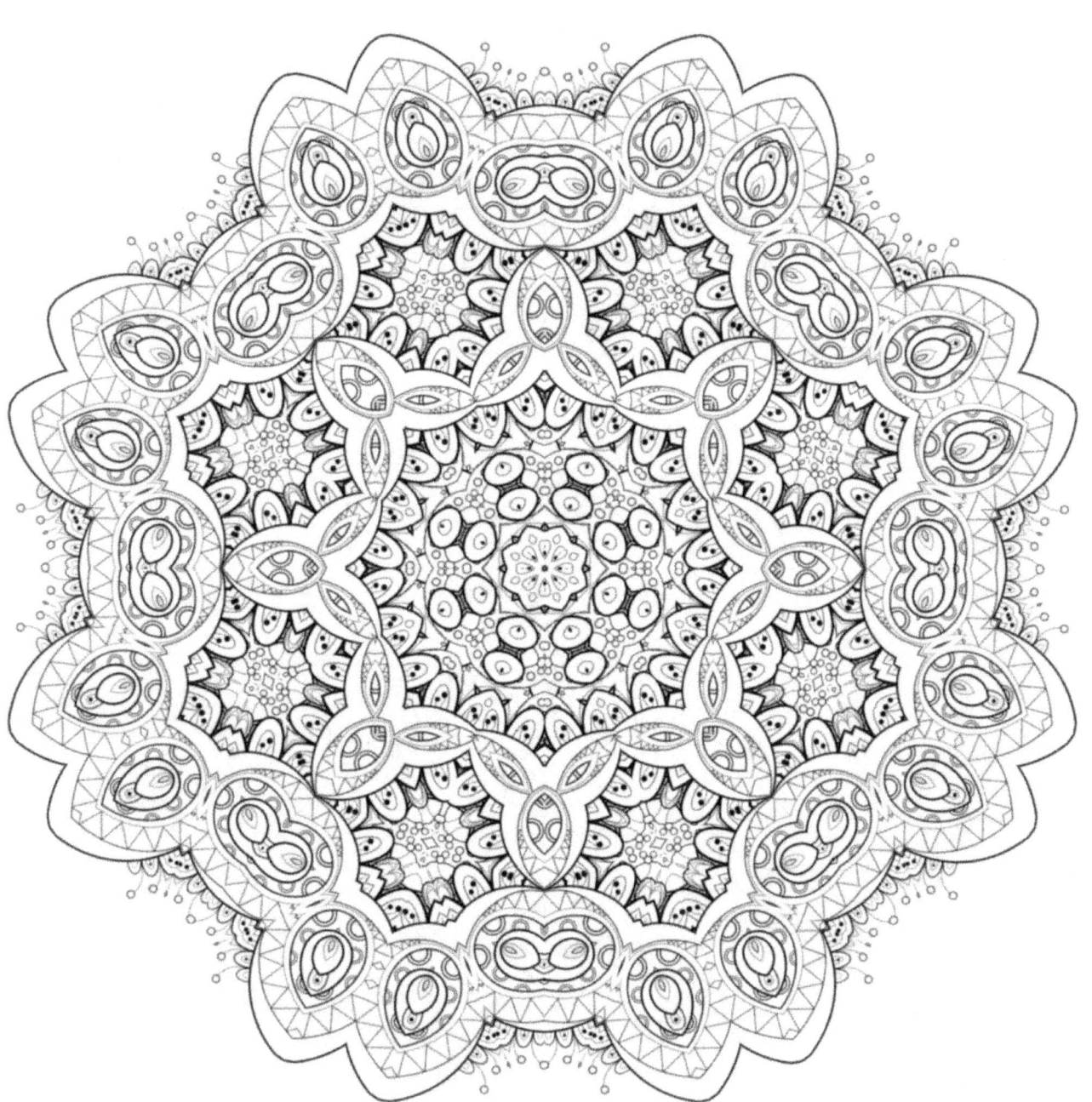

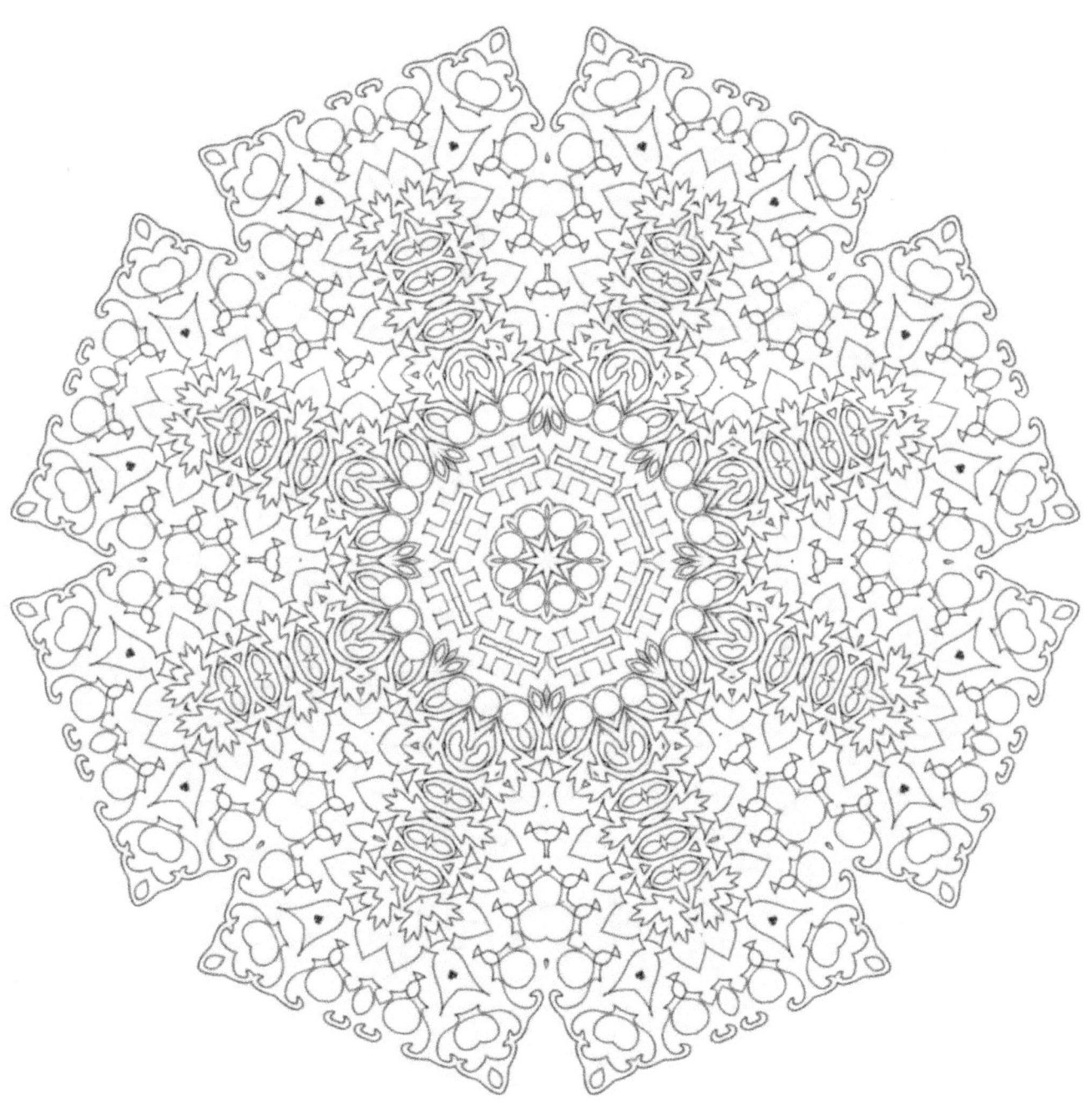

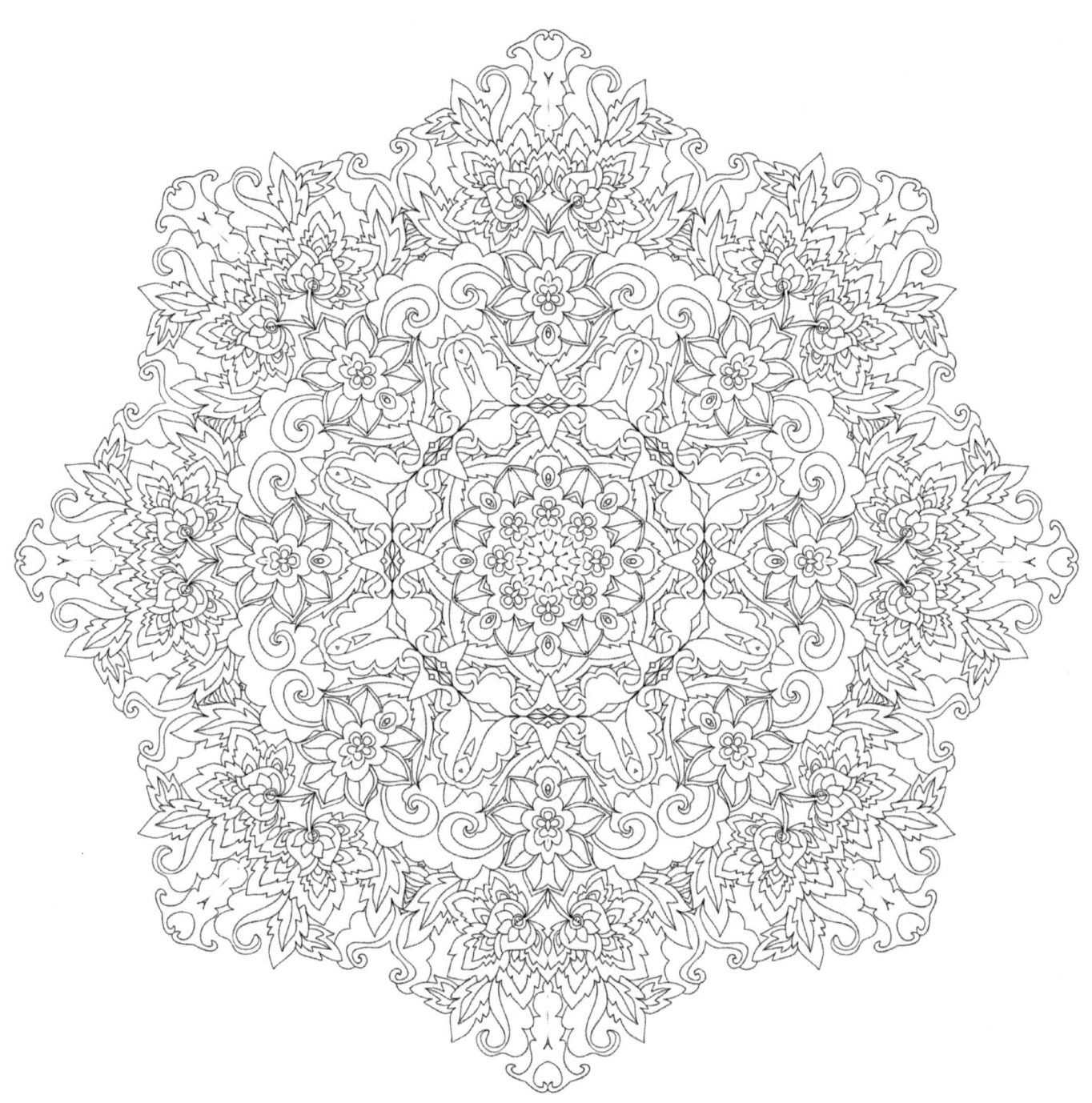

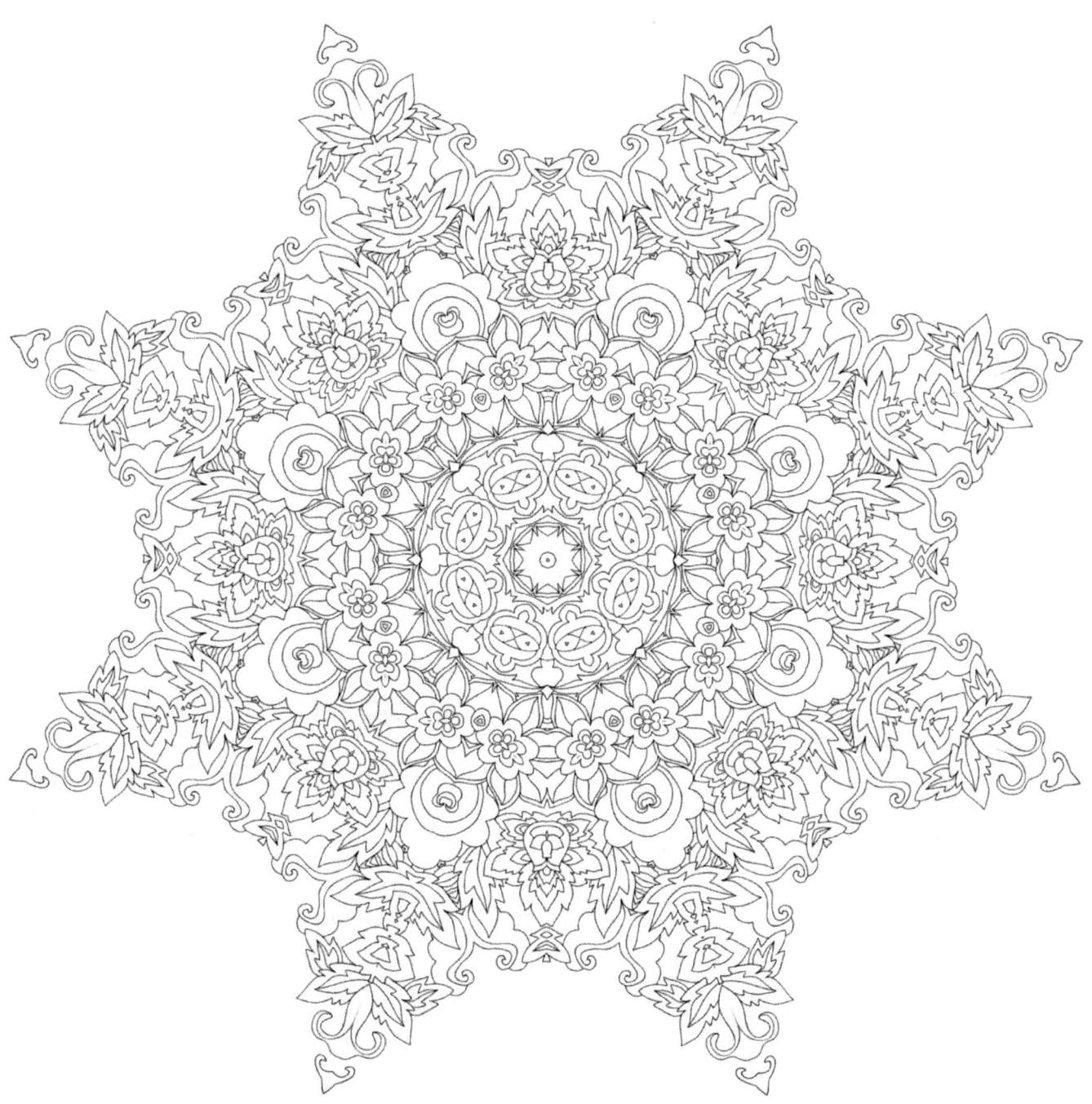

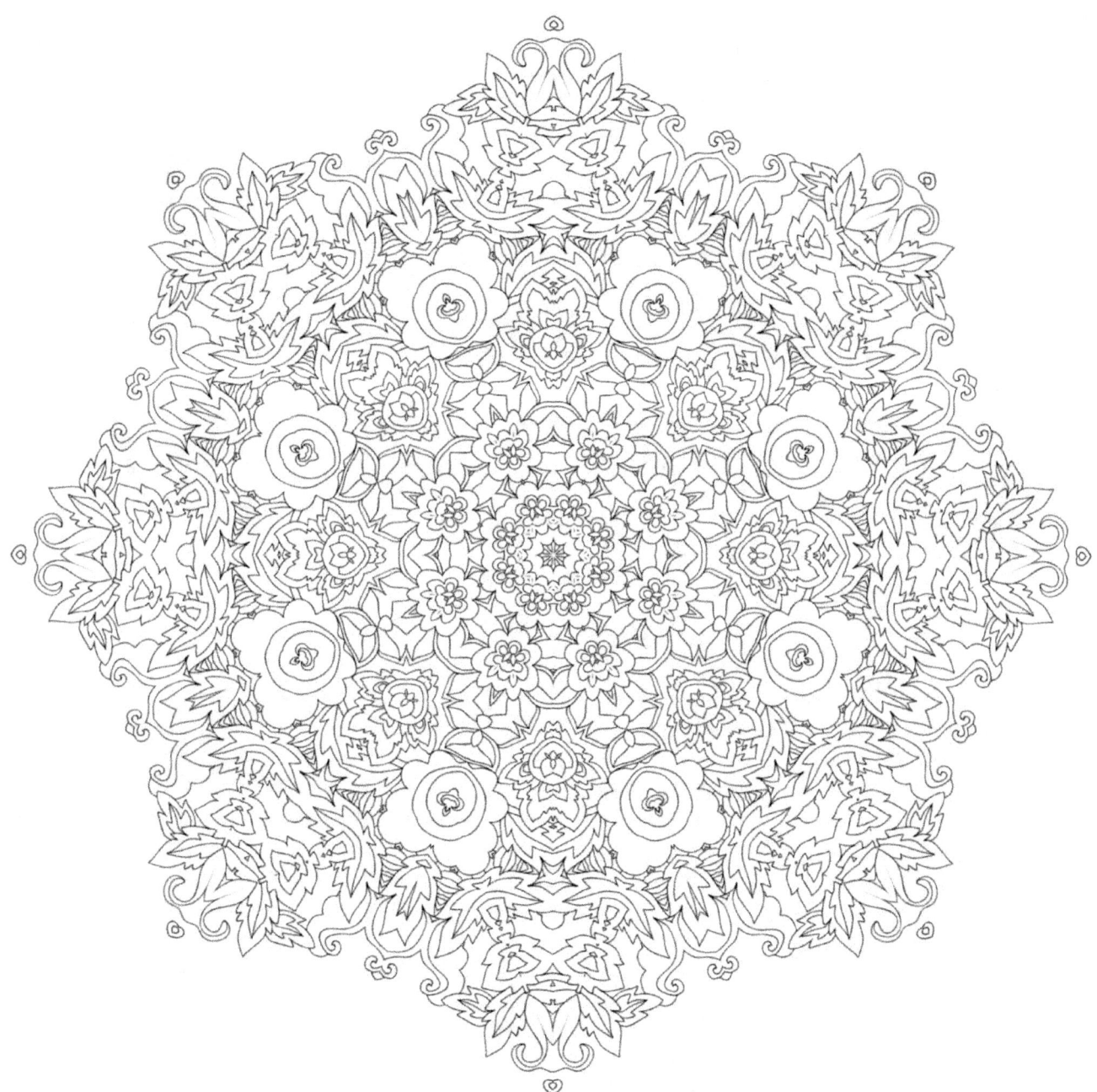

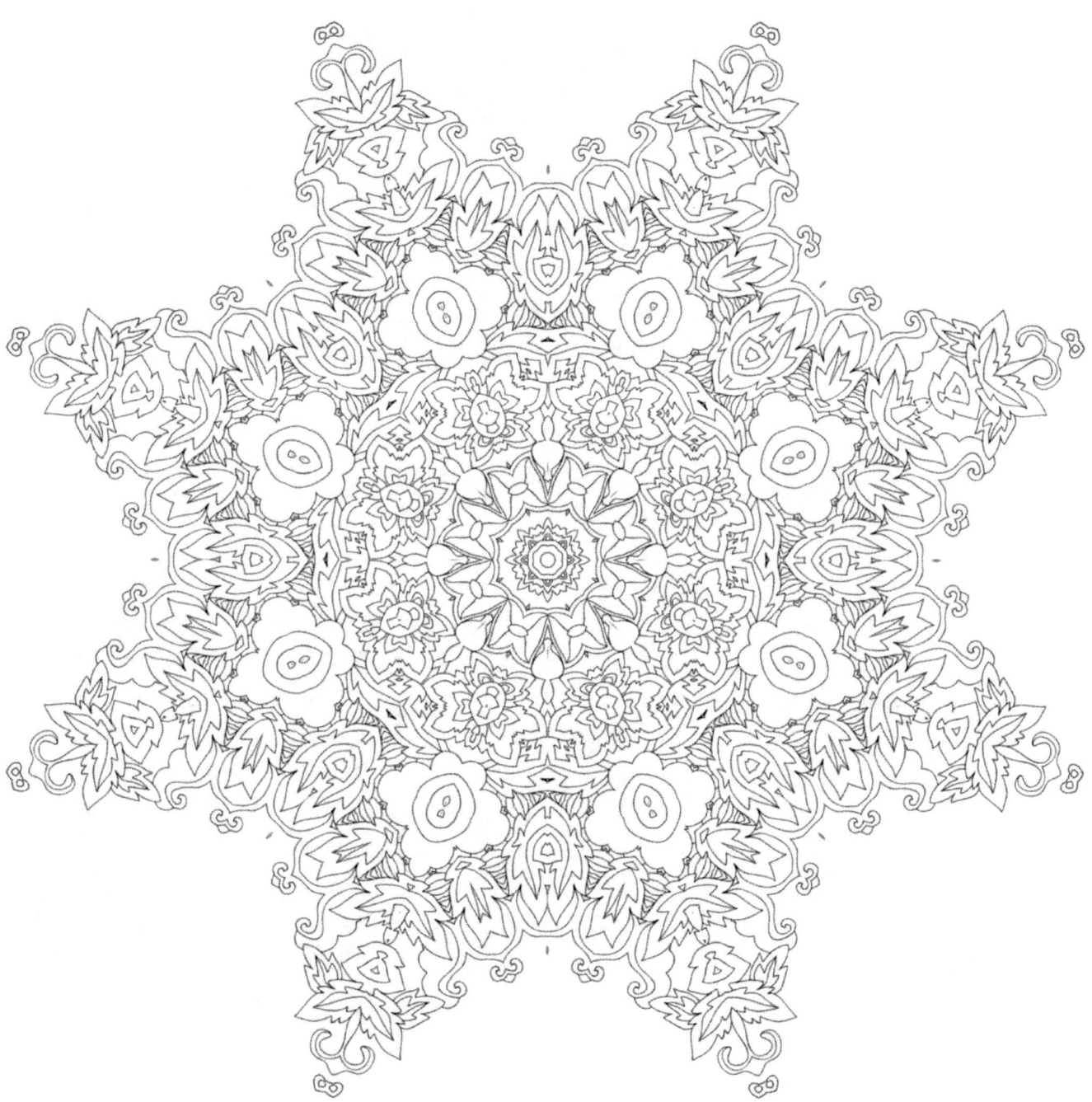

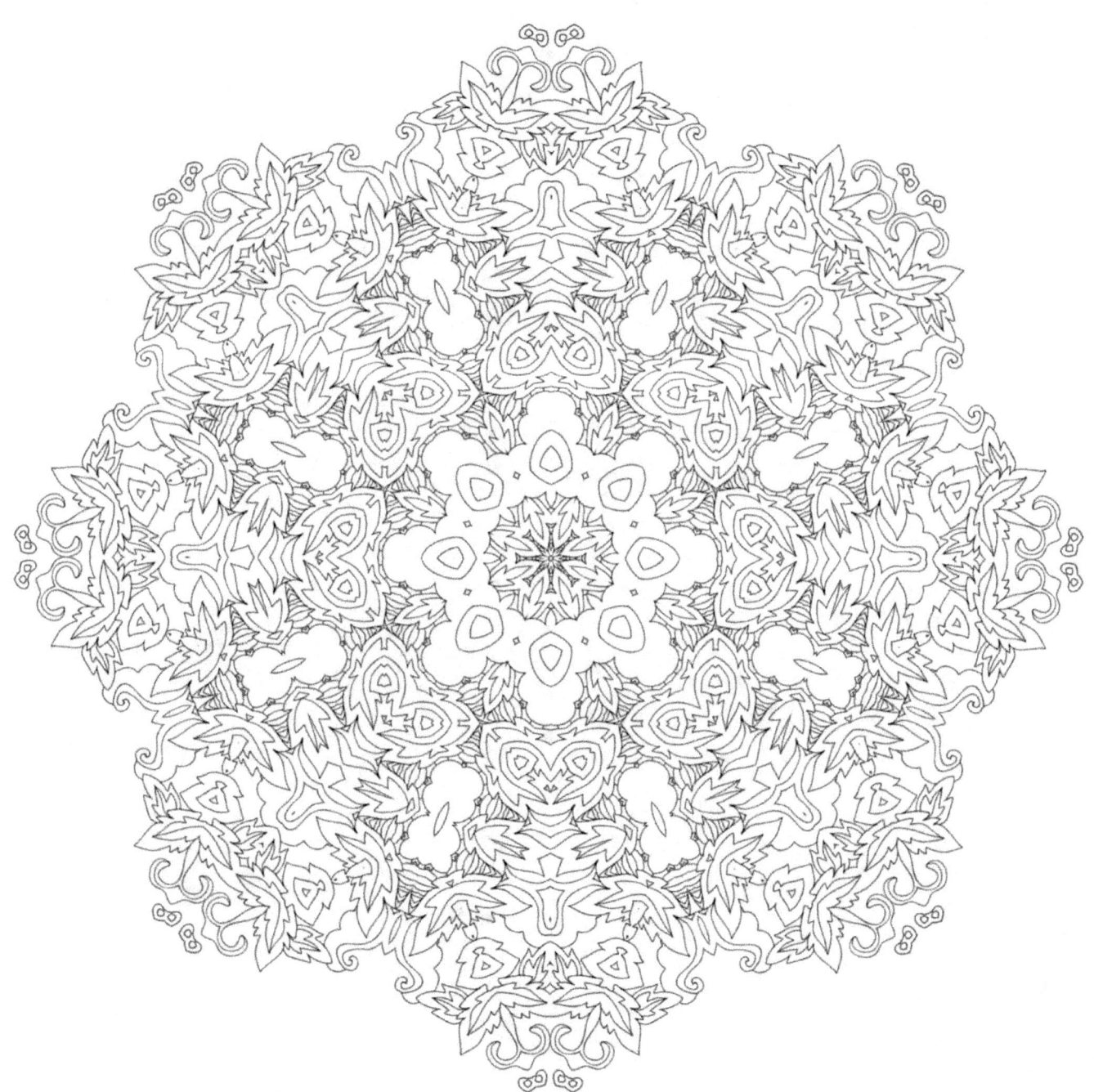

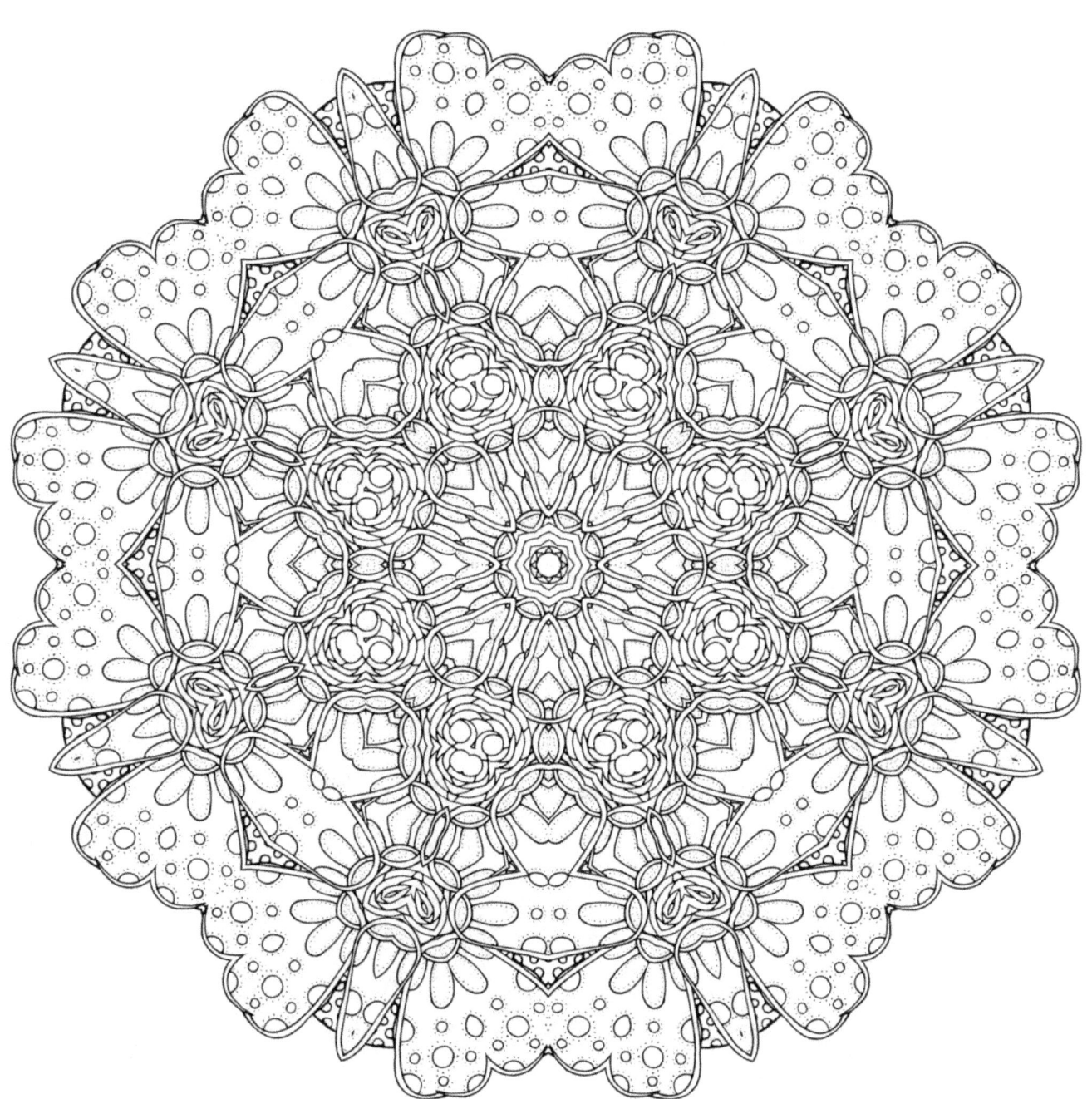

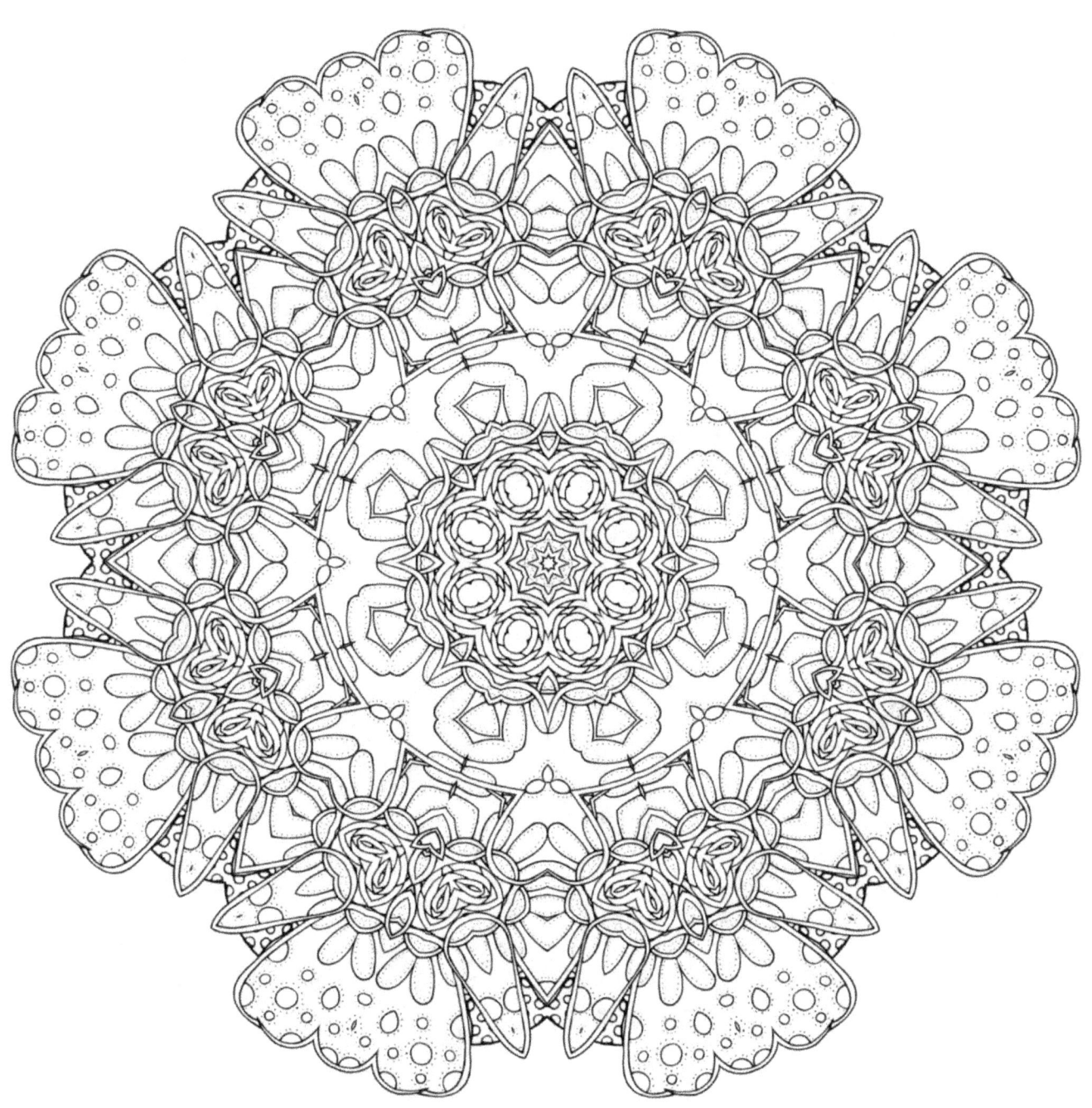

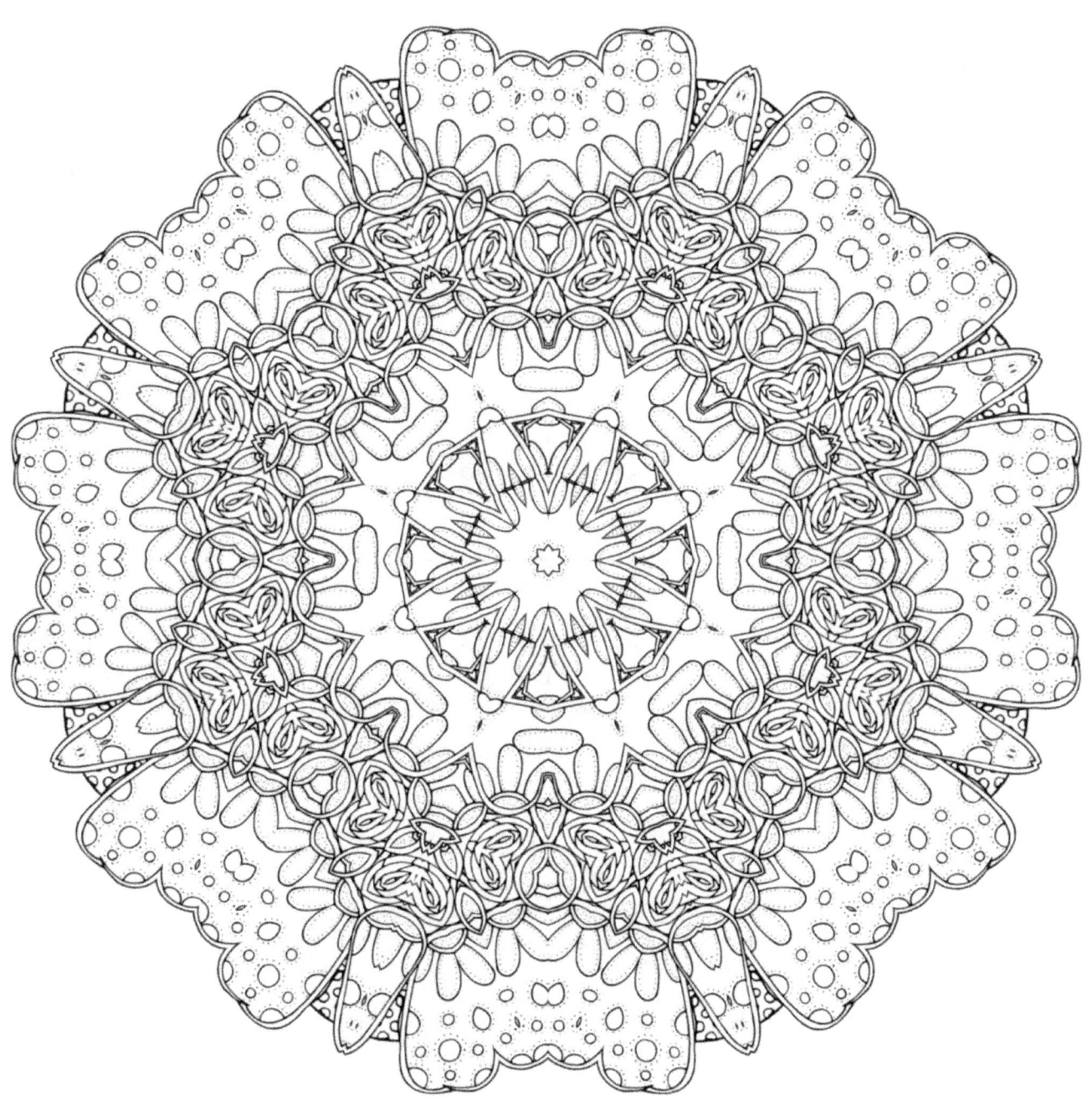

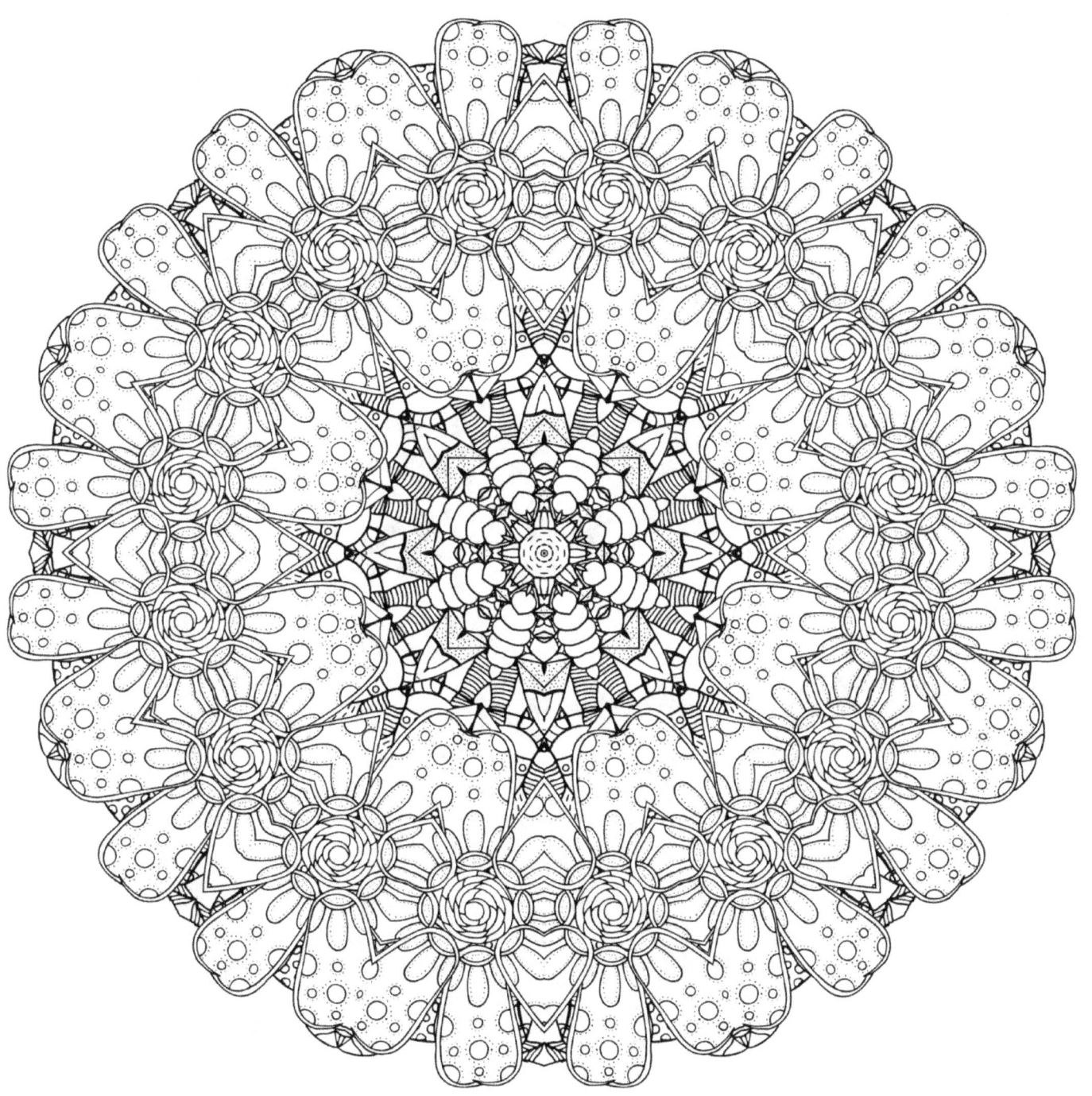

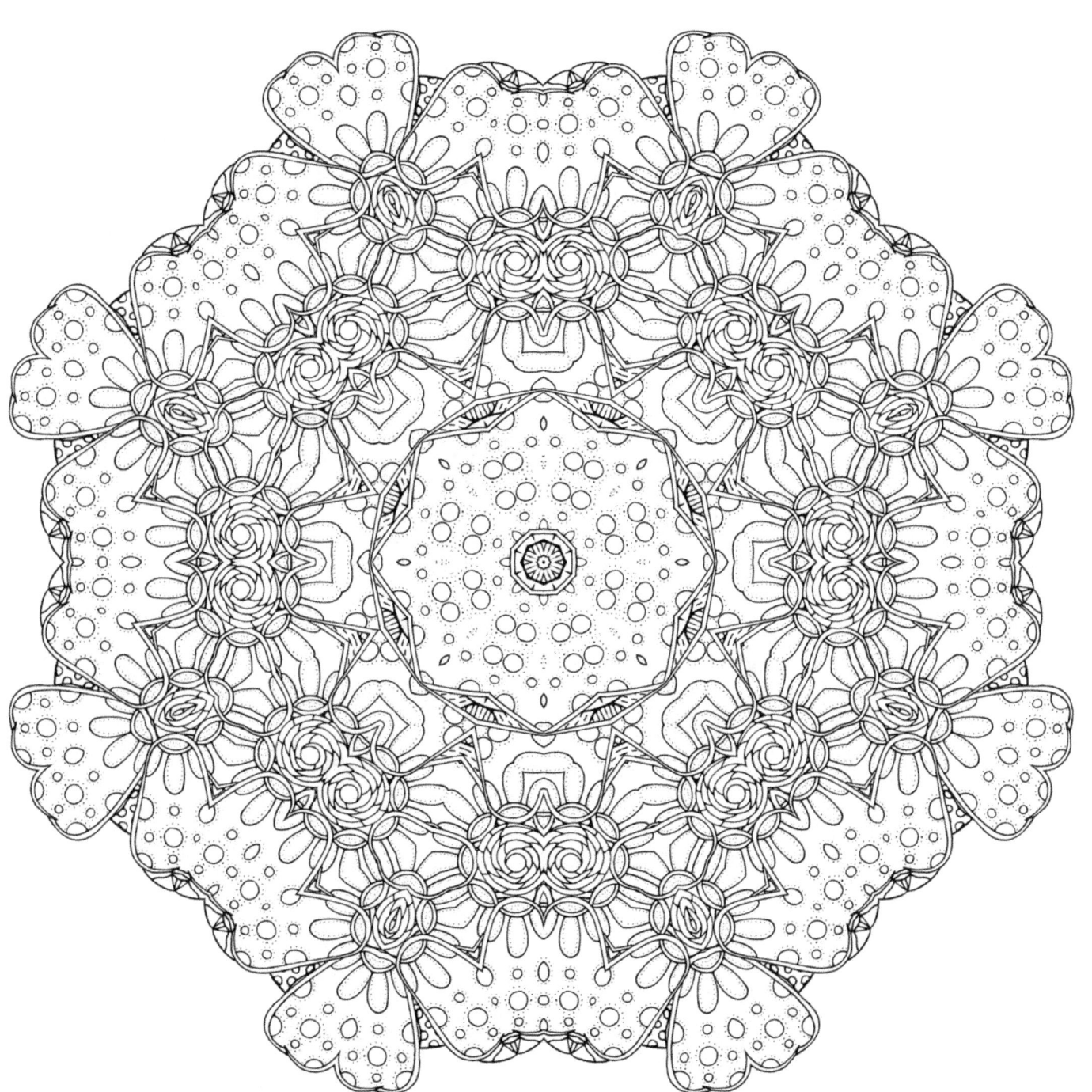

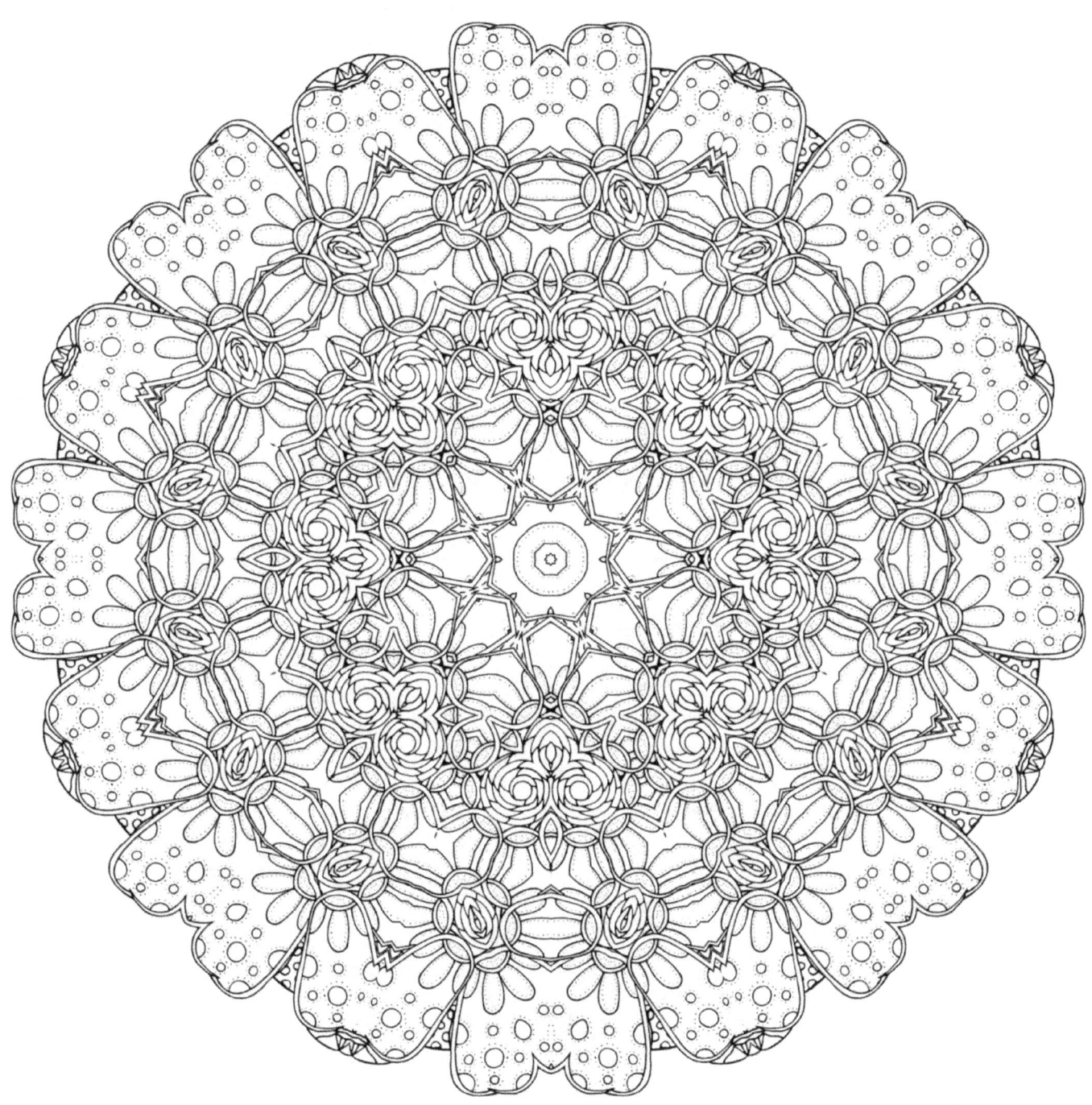

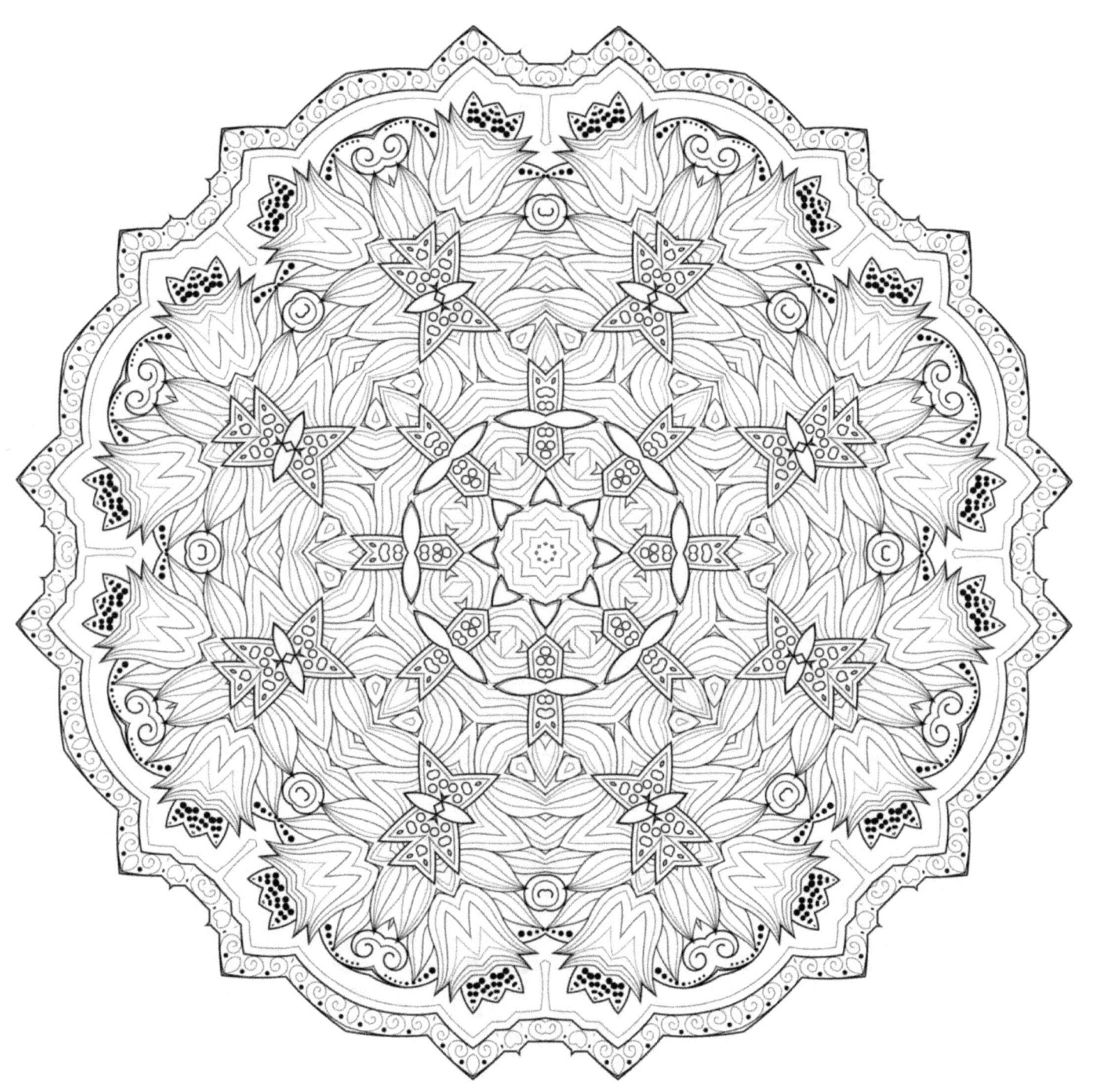

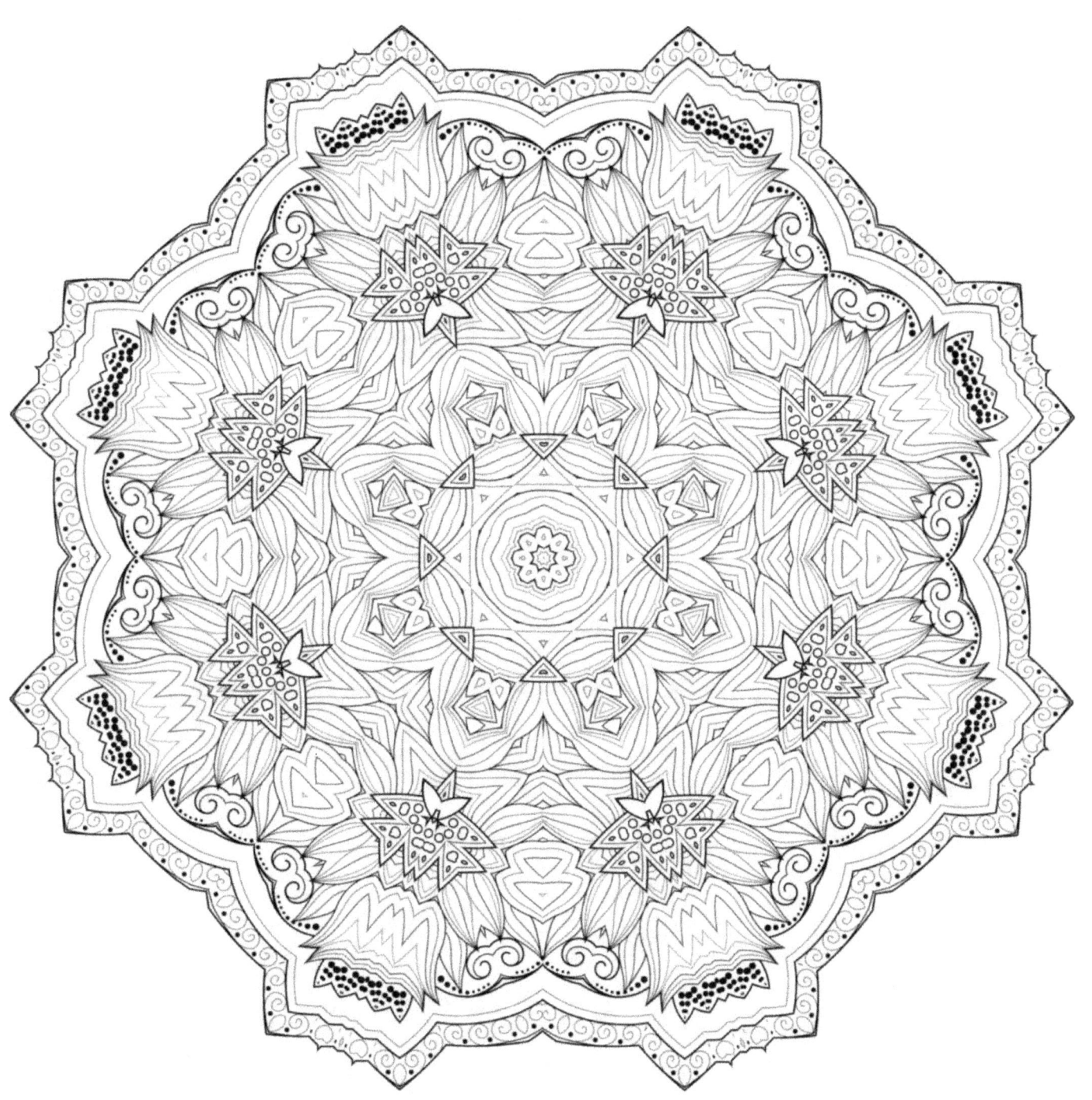

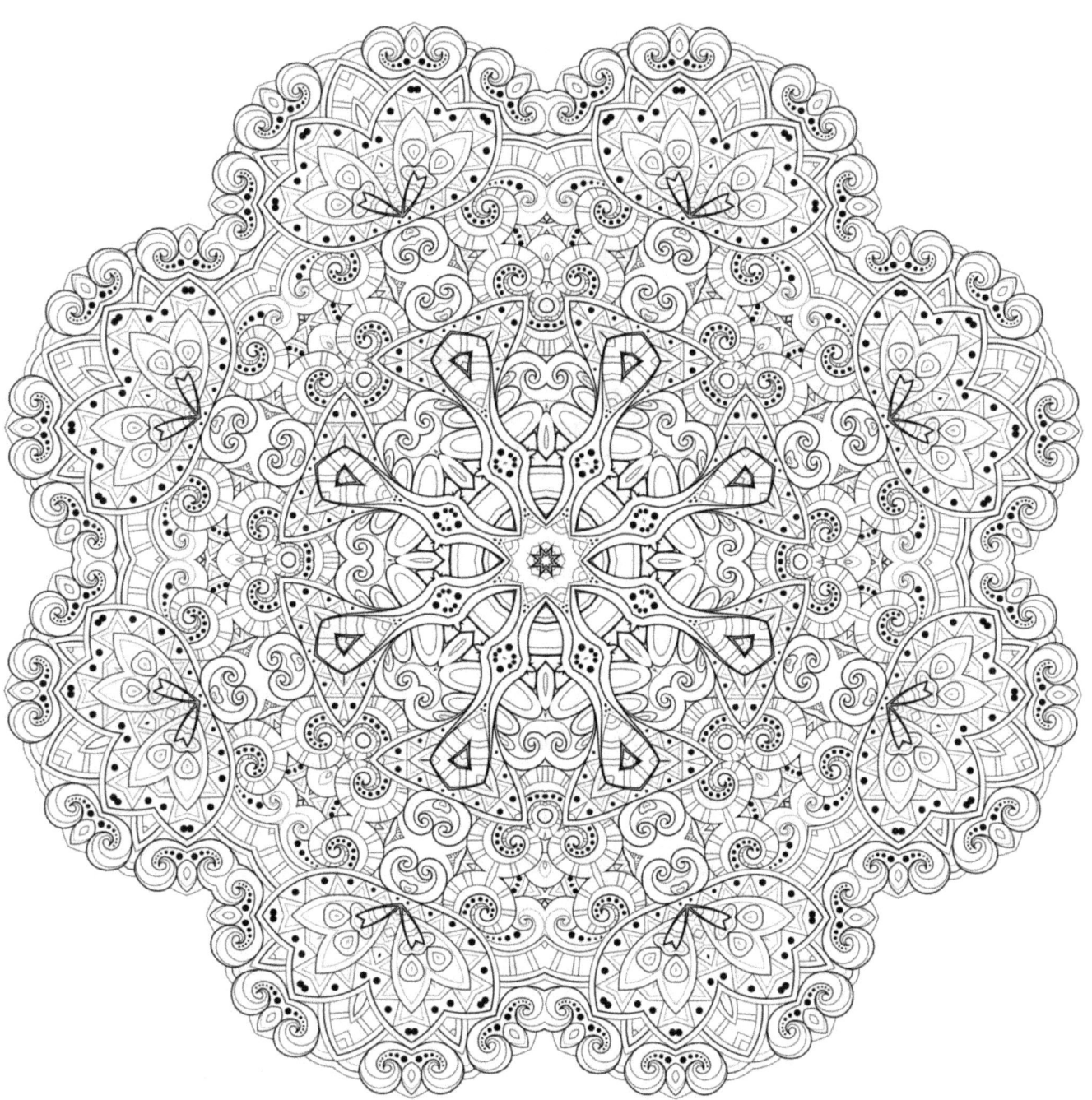

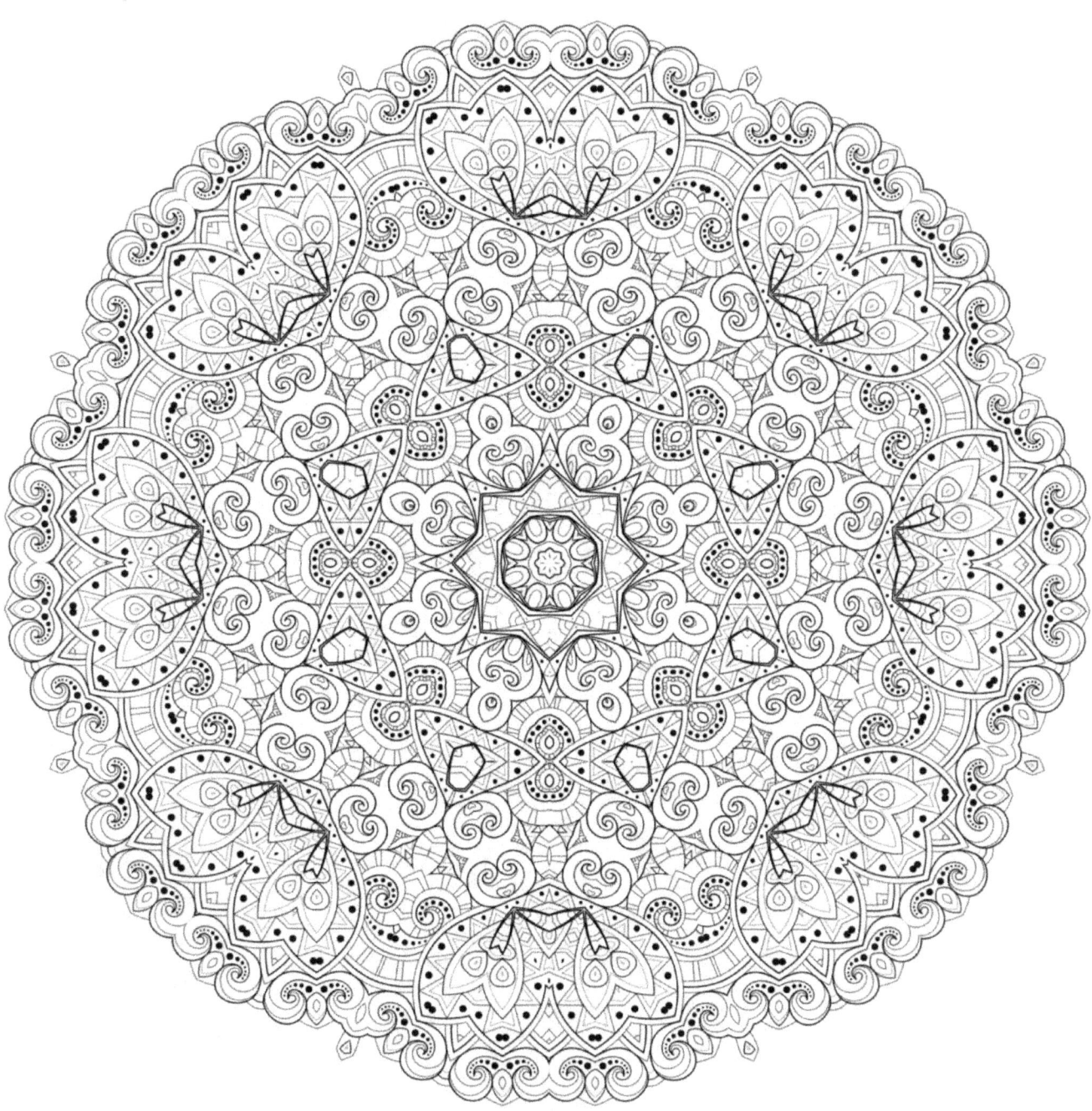

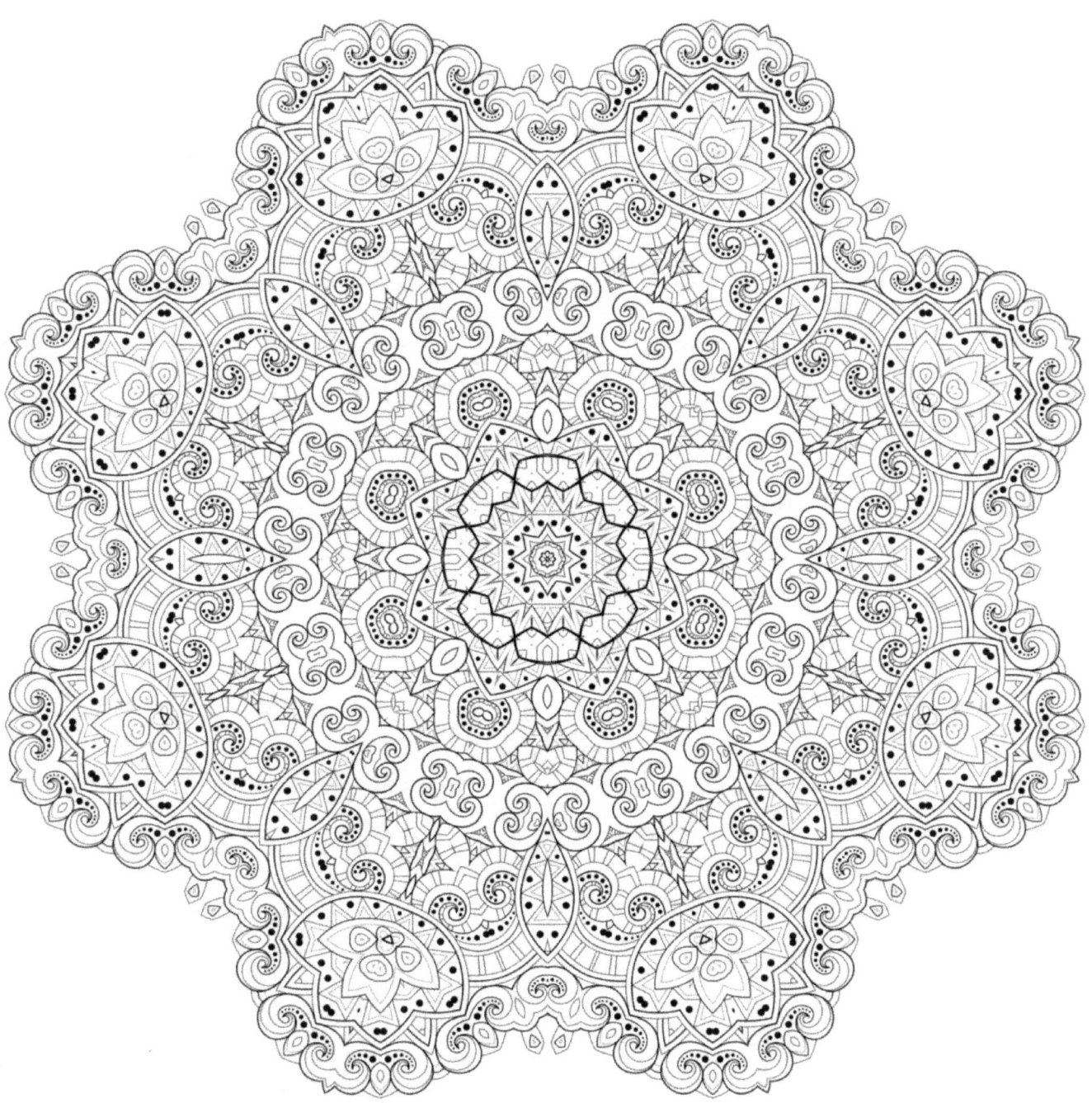

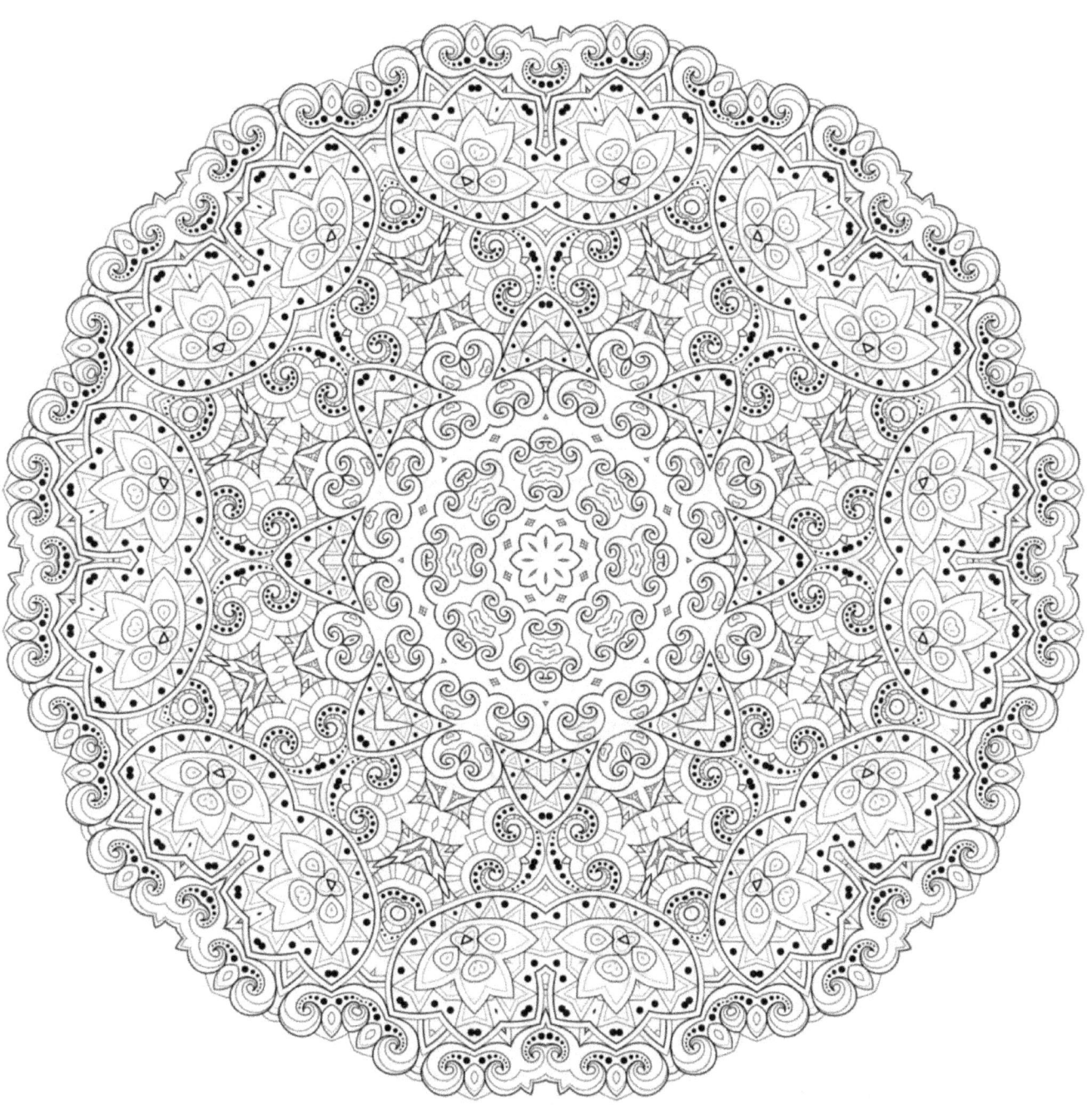

www.ingramcontent.com/pod-product-compliance
Lightning Source LLC
Chambersburg PA
CBHW081610170526
45166CB00009B/2909